CHRIST YESHUA ALONE:
The Answer to Your Nagging Questions

VINCE AMAECHI

Copyright © 2013 by Vince Amaechi

Christ Yeshua Alone: The Answer to Your Nagging Questions
by Vince Amaechi

2nd Edition

Printed in the United States of America

ISBN 9781626973640

All rights reserved solely by the author. The author guarantees all contents are original and do not infringe upon the legal rights of any other person or work. No part of this book may be reproduced in any form without the permission of the author. The views expressed in this book are not necessarily those of the publisher.

Unless otherwise marked, all Scripture quotations are taken from the New King James Version (NKJV). Copyright © 1982 by Thomas Nelson, Inc. Used by permission. All rights reserved; New American Standard Bible (NASB). Copyright © 1960, 1962, 1963, 1968, 1971, 1972, 1973, 1975, 1977, 1995 by The Lockman Foundation. Used by permission. All rights reserved.

KJV—King James Version

Amplified Bible (AMP). Copyright © 1954, 1958, 1962, 1964, 1965, 1987 by The Lockman Foundation. Used by permission. All rights reserved.

New Living Translation (NLT). Copyright © 1996, 2004, 2007 by Tyndale House Foundation. Used by permission. All rights reserved.

New American Standard Bible (NASB). Copyright © 1960, 1962, 1963, 1968, 1971, 1972, 1973, 1975, 1977, 1995 by The Lockman Foundation. Used by permission. All rights reserved.

www.xulonpress.com

Contents

Dedication vii

Acknowledgements ix

Chapter 9 11
1. Christ Yeshua Alone 13
2. Focused Commitment, Blind Obedience . . 26

Chapter 10 35
3. Labourers of the Kingdom 37
4. The Authority in the Word 47

Chapter 11 59
5. Teach us to Pray 61
6. What More do You Want? 71
7. Outside Versus Inside 84

Chapter 12 97
8. Poor, Rich Hypocrite 99
9. Stop Worrying, Keep Watching 111
10. Prince of Peace; Lord of Division 124

Chapter 13. 139
11. Lord, Why Me? 141

DEDICATION

―❦―

*I am dedicating this book to
Mr Robert Oku, my father in the Lord,
who did not know, until I visited him in 2008,
that the invitation he gave me in 1976 to attend
a
gospel concert resulted in my getting born-again
and becoming a Christian.
I am so much indebted to him for persisting
and not giving up on me.*

Acknowledgements

I would like to thank those of you who have read the previous volumes of this series of commentaries, and have shared with me how much you have enjoyed reading them. Many have remarked that it is imperative for the rest of the volumes to be published as soon as possible.

I would also like to thank Miss Beryl Nartey, my secretary at the time I was writing this volume, who did the tedious job of deciphering my handwriting from the manuscripts and typing them out to what you are reading today.

Finally, I want to thank my wife, Ogoma and my children, Chinoge, Daberechi, Obuineke, Ngozi and Ozioma, for being there for me and giving me the strength and morale boost that was needed for doing these writings.

Thank you all and may God bless you.

Luke Chapter 9

1

CHRIST YESHUA ALONE

―✿✿―

Luke 9:23-36

We live in a world full of policies, guidelines, rules and regulations; with all sorts of risk assessments for all sorts of situations. In almost every area of work, there are governing documents that determine every undertaking. The purpose of all these is to ensure a safe and comfortable environment for work.

For instance, risk assessments are conducted to help pre-empt all occurrences of risk and their consequences, whether they are high, medium or low risks. After due consideration, necessary controls to minimise the hazards are sought to be in place. To live in this world, risks need to be taken, but with foresight and proper checks, high risks can become low or insignificant risks.

In today's study, the Lord Yeshua acknowledges that the world is full of hazards—high, medium and low risks—and that we have to take risks with great controls in place. However, He reveals that the control we need is Him, Yeshua and Yeshua alone. So, we'll be looking at the subject of Yeshua and Yeshua alone.

Let's take a reading from Luke 9:23-36.

[23]Then He said to them all, "If anyone desires to come after Me, let him deny himself, and take up his cross daily, and follow Me. [24]For whoever desires to save his life will lose it, but whoever loses his life for My sake will save it. [25]For what profit is it to a man if he gains the whole world, and is himself destroyed or lost? [26]For whoever is ashamed of Me and My words, of him the Son of Man will be ashamed when He comes in His own glory, and in His Father's, and of the holy angels.

[27]But I tell you truly, there are some standing here who shall not taste death till they see the kingdom of God." [28]Now it came to pass, about eight days after these sayings, that He took Peter, John, and James and went up on the mountain to pray. [29] As He prayed, the appearance of His face was altered and His robe became white and glistening. [30]And behold, two men talked with Him, who were Moses and Elijah, [31]who appeared in glory and spoke of His decease which He was about to accomplish at Jerusalem.

[32]But Peter and those with him were heavy with sleep; and when they were fully awake, they saw His glory and the two men who stood with Him. [33]Then it happened, as they were parting from Him, that Peter said to Jesus,

"Master, it is good for us to be here; and let us make three tabernacles: one for You, one for Moses, and one for Elijah"—not knowing what he said. ³⁴While he was saying this, a cloud came and overshadowed them; and they were fearful as they entered the cloud. ³⁵And a voice came out of the cloud, saying, "This is My beloved Son. Hear Him!" ³⁶When the voice had ceased, Jesus was found alone. But they kept quiet, and told no one in those days any of the things they had seen.

(Luke 9:23-36)

Health and Safety policies are guiding principles that help us to protect our lives and the lives of others around us. They inform us about things that could harm us internally and make us aware of adverse external forces as well.

The Lord, however, would like us to know that there is no other health and safety precaution in the world other than Christ Yeshua alone. People will do whatever it takes to preserve their lives, but without Jesus there efforts will be futile; there will be no health and there will be no safety. All your risk assessments will all be a waste of time without Yeshua.

Whether you are making a whole lot of sacrifice for mankind or living for self, without the Lord Yeshua, your soul would be lost. If you are ashamed of the Lord today, He will be ashamed of you later. It may be too late. In all these, it is Christ Yeshua alone.

He is your risk assessment. He is your only Health & Safety check.

We will learn from the above passage that if we want to follow Christ and be His disciples, we would need to undergo some form of transfiguration, not just physically but also spiritually.

Transfiguration:

Of Christ

The Lord took his select disciples to a mountaintop where he was transfigured before them. They did not go there for an open-air picnic, for fireworks or a magic show. He took them for a deep teaching journey that would eventually transform the rest of their lives. He was taking them to a level far beyond what they had experienced in their lives. The question is why did He do this?

When the Lord Yeshua came into this world, He was not really well-known or understood by the people. Even some of His followers doubted Him. He, therefore, had to take them to the place of transfiguration, beyond the point between the physical and the metaphysical; between what is seen and what is not visible; between what they knew and the things that were beyond their knowledge.

The Lord took them through this experience to show them his glory. He wanted them to believe in Him strongly. For Moses and Elijah, iconic characters that represented the Law and the Prophets, to appear and talk with Him was enough to make the most ardent critic think twice.

Of us
The significance of the transfiguration was not just for the Lord Yeshua, the Christ, to show his power and glory but for the benefit of the disciples and those who would believe after them. The encounter reveals the awesome magnitude of our redemption and fellowship with Christ. It also teaches us that in every sphere of life, there are degrees and levels. Concerning this, Christianity is no exception.

There are times to seek God on a higher level. There are also times God will choose to take you up on a higher level, not necessarily for what you have done. If we diligently seek Him, He will transform our lives. Sometimes, He will do it to move us from our comfort zone.

Retirement
The Lord also used the mountain experience to teach the disciples about the need for a place away from the daily hustle and bustle of life, to a place of prayer and communion with God.

The mount of transfiguration

A place where Christ will shine radiantly through your life.

A place of knowing your Moses and your Elijah.

A place of knowing your laws and your prophets.

It was as if the Lord was saying, "You would need to take some time off and retreat to a place like this, a place of transfiguration and a place to search the Scriptures. During these times in the Word you will find prophesies written concerning me. That is what Moses and Elijah are here to confirm. They are not here to speak about themselves but about ME, because it's Me, Christ Yeshua alone."

How Long Will I Stay With You?

Have you ever watched the face of a teacher who has an active class of hungry learners, students who want to develop and grow? A class of active, reactive and interactive students? Teachers love this kind of class. The students ask a lot of questions. They show interest in what they are taught. These kind of students or disciples gladden the heart and brighten the face of their teacher. They prove to him that they can do what he had been teaching them to do.

Whether it is Primary, Secondary or University education; in business, at home or any other walk of life; teachers love to see their pupils putting into practice what they had learnt.

Some teachers even go as far as giving incentives to their students, something to keep them interested in and focused on learning. The teacher aims to pass on themselves, their very soul, into the lives of the learners.

This said, you can understand the frustration a teacher endures when all his efforts seem not to produce the desired result. Some certainly feel like coming down on their students: "How long will I have to teach you before you get it? How many more times do I have to go over this same problem?"

That's exactly what happened with the passage we are going to look at in Luke 9:37-50.

³⁷Now it happened on the next day, when they had come down from the mountain, that a great multitude met Him. ³⁸Suddenly a man from the multitude cried out, saying, "Teacher, I implore You, look on my son, for he is my only child. ³⁹And behold, a spirit seizes him, and he suddenly cries out; it convulses him so that he foams at the mouth; and it departs from him with great difficulty, bruising him. ⁴⁰So I implored Your disciples to cast it out, but they could not." ⁴¹Then Jesus answered and said, "O faithless and perverse generation, how long shall I be with you and bear with you? Bring your son here." ⁴²And as he was still coming, the demon threw him down and convulsed him. Then Jesus rebuked the unclean spirit, healed the child, and gave him back to his father.

⁴³And they were all amazed at the majesty of God. But while everyone marveled at all the things which Jesus did, He said to His disciples, ⁴⁴"Let these words sink down into your ears, for the Son of Man is about to be betrayed into the hands of men." ⁴⁵But they did not understand this saying, and it was hidden from them so that they did not perceive it; and they were afraid to ask Him about this saying.

⁴⁶Then a dispute arose among them as to which of them would be greatest. ⁴⁷And

Jesus, perceiving the thought of their heart, took a little child and set him by Him, [48]and said to them, "Whoever receives this little child in My name receives Me; and whoever receives Me receives Him who sent Me. For he who is least among you all will be great."

[49]Now John answered and said, "Master, we saw someone casting out demons in Your name, and we forbade him because he does not follow with us." [50]But Jesus said to him, "Do not forbid him, for he who is not against us is on our side."

(Luke 9:37-50)

Yeshua, the Messiah, was rebuking His disciples: "What's the matter with you? How long will I stay with you before you grasp the basic principles of who you are? From now on you are the children of God, the Creator. You are my disciples, appointed to do my work. People know you as a church person, but when are you going to grow up and be a disciple? When are you going to mature and begin to do the works of the Master?" These same questions He is asking us today.
Read Luke 9:37-50 again.
"How long will I be with you?"
Verses 37-40 teaches us that:
- the world is full of trouble, trials and temptation.
- the enemy is tormenting people everywhere — his normal job of killing, stealing and destroying lives.

- most of the time he does not give up unless we bring the Lord Yeshua into the picture.

Nevertheless, no matter how much the enemy has oppressed you or made you scream in pain, declare it today, that at the name of Yeshua the Messiah, you are set free indeed.

Verse 38 tells us that we have got to be bold and not ashamed when approaching Yeshua with our needs and infirmities. This man was not embarrassed at all; he was desperate to grab Yeshua's attention. He cried out in desperation. You can do the same.

Again, verses 38-40 teaches that even when we do not fully know who we are or the full strength of our calling as disciples of the Lord, the world around us will not stop having expectations of us. Whether we know it or not, people have the notion that we are capable of doing extraordinary things; things that ordinary people are not able to do.

"Where did you get that funny idea from?" you may be thinking. Well, an apprentice is expected to develop and become like his master. A car maintenance apprentice, when fully trained, will be able to repair cars to the same standard as his trainer. Medical students learn with a bid to become competent doctors. Likewise, as disciples of the Lord Yeshua, his disciples (apprentices) were expected to have learnt how to do the things He was able to do.

In other words, the people presumed that the disciples could heal the sick, cast out demons and demonstrate the Kingdom of God. However, the expectation of the man in this story was dashed when the disciples could not 'perform' like their Master.

The Lord Yeshua himself was disappointed with His disciples. He rebuked them sternly in verse 41, ***"O faithless and perverse generation, how long shall I be with you and bear with you? Bring your son here."***

It is almost like the Lord was saying: "Oh, you unbelieving bunch, how long do I still have to be with you and put up with your unbelief? When are you going to grow up in your faith? How long do you think I am going to be here with you? It is time you grow up and realise who you are and start doing what you're called to do. I have promised that I will never leave nor forsake you. Just ask whatever you need, in my name, and I will grant it to you. Now, move aside and let me show you. . . Bring the boy here to me!"

Verse 42

The people were all amazed at the greatness of God. It is not about you, child of God; it is about God. Miracles, signs and wonders are given to display the greatness of God, so that people will see His power and give Him praise, and not us.

Verses 43-45

The Lord was here teaching His disciples to stop living in denial. He discerned that they were of the mind that He was never going to leave them; that he was not going to fall into the hands of his persecutors and be killed. The Lord confronted this by saying, "Let these words sink right deep into your heart; whether you like it or not, it is going to happen."

Verses 46-47

One of the reasons why some of us fail to do what is expected of us is the presence of too much power struggle. The Lord Yeshua is teaching His disciples what He came for and what they should be doing when He leaves them physically. They heard him but they didn't want to accept it. They found it difficult to understand and did not want any clarification.

Why? Because they were happy with the status quo. They were happy the way things were. They had already mapped out in their heads how famous they would be when they manage to overpower their Roman captors. As a matter of fact, they were already celebrities just by being with the Lord Yeshua for three years.

So, they were saying: "we don't want to know about this going away business. We don't want to hear you talking about death. If it ever happens, who is going to be President or Prime minister? Who is going to be the Chancellor of the Exchequer? Who's going to be the Foreign Secretary, who's going to be the Secretary of State?"

They thought the whole thing was about them. What about you, dear reader? It is true that Yeshua has called and chosen you, but His mission is not all about you. There are still millions out there who still do not know Him. There are still the poor and the needy who need you as His representative.

Dear Apostle of God
Dear disciple of Yeshua
Dearly beloved child of God
"It's not about yourself"

Says – Yeshua the Messiah.
"Remove personal pursuit
If you want to serve Me."

In verse 47 the Lord Yeshua showed that He knew what was in their hearts. He knows what is in our hearts and can see our thoughts from afar.

Verses 48-49
1. He encourages us to be humble – like little children. He encourages us not to be selfish.
2. He admonishes us to steer clear of envy and jealousy.
3. To stay away from strife and dissention if we are going to do his business.

The Lord Yeshua says, "How long do I have to tell you this before you grasp it? My coming is not all about you. The Gospel is not just about you. There are many out there who would like to hear it. They have great expectations of you, my disciples, what you are supposed to be?"

Verse 50 says, Do not be a hindrance. Do not be an obstacle to the preaching of the Gospel. Do not block the flow of miracles, signs and wonders. You will be a stumbling block when you focus only on yourself, what you want to be and those who are with you. Definitely, if they are not against you, they must be for you.

The Lord said to them, "How long will I be with you before you really understand that it's about Me and Me alone and how I want you to display the glory and the greatness of God in your lives?"

May this be our vision today, in Yeshua's name.

2

FOCUSED COMMITMENT THROUGH BLIND OBEDIENCE

―∞―

Luke 9:51-62

Have you ever met with devoted Muslims? You will notice that they have a commitment through blind obedience. In fact, this is evident among Hindus too or many other religions. These groups believe that for anyone to be a true member, they must have focused commitment through blind obedience.

Even among Roman Catholics, Jehovah's Witnesses and other religious movements, this kind of commitment is evident. Indeed, any true follower of Yeshua must demonstrate focused commitment through blind obedience. This is what the Lord Yeshua is teaching in the next segment of our study.

> [51]Now it came to pass, when the time had come for Him to be received up, that He steadfastly set His face to go to Jerusalem, [52]and sent messengers before His face. And as they went, they entered a village of the

Samaritans, to prepare for Him. [53]But they did not receive Him, because His face was set for the journey to Jerusalem. [54]And when His disciples James and John saw this, they said, "Lord, do You want us to command fire to come down from heaven and consume them, just as Elijah did?"[55]But He turned and rebuked them, and said, "You do not know what manner of spirit you are of. [56]For the Son of Man did not come to destroy men's lives but to save them." And they went to another village.

[57]Now it happened as they journeyed on the road, that someone said to Him, "Lord, I will follow You wherever You go." [58]And Jesus said to him, "Foxes have holes and birds of the air have nests, but the Son of Man has nowhere to lay His head." [59]Then He said to another, "Follow Me." But he said, "Lord, let me first go and bury my father." [60]Jesus said to him, Let the dead bury their own dead, but you go and preach the kingdom of God." [61]And another also said, "Lord, I will follow You, but let me first go and bid them farewell who are at my house." [62]But Jesus said to him, "No one, having put his hand to the plow, and looking back, is fit for the kingdom of God."

(Luke 9:51-62)

No ifs, no buts

Verses 51-56

In this passage, the Lord Yeshua uses Himself as an example to teach us about focused commitment. He knew what awaited Him in Jerusalem but was committed to fulfilling His mission. He was not going to allow any distraction, neither was he going to lose the focus of what he had come to do. No amount of pain, shame or loss could make him give up on completing His mandate.

The Bible did not talk about the suffering of Yeshua here, what He was going to face in Jerusalem, but simply said, *"Now when the time was almost come for Yeshua to be received up to heaven."* As far as God was concerned, the issue was not the pain and suffering of Yeshua, but the result and fruit of His obedience. The Holy Spirit who inspired Luke's writing, concentrated on the time that was coming when He would be received back into heaven having conquered death and Satan.

What does this teach us? God values focused commitment to service through blind obedience to his word. This is why we should consider the sufferings of this present age to be nothing compared to the glory that is going to be revealed in us (Romans 8:18). This is also why the Bible, in this passage, did not bother talking about the pain of that present time, but focused on the glory that will be His when He is received back into heaven.

The Bible does not deny the presence of pain and suffering, but encourages us to be fully focused and committed to obeying God's word, in the face of them. Let's look at some distractions that can derail us from being focused on and committed to God.

Verse 52
A Samaritan village refused to receive Yeshua.
· They did not believe in Him. They did not know anything about His mission.
· Even if they knew, they did not want to get involved or be linked with someone well-known as a "trouble-maker."
· They could not understand someone who could stare at death in the face; someone who had massive powers but still kept on saying, "In a few days time I will be handed over to the leaders of our land and be killed."

The Samaritans considered it madness, a type they had never seen before. They did not want to be seen as supporters of such a notorious subversive element.

Actually, they were afraid of supporting the truth; they did not want to get into trouble.

Have you seen such situations in your life; where people deny you – or even speak against you – in order to join the gang and not be the odd ones out? How painful that must have been for the Lord Yeshua. They denied Him. They denied his mission. They didn't want to get into trouble. That incident was enough to distract and derail Him. He could have thrown away the baby with the bath water and start chasing the shadows of revenge rather than the mission of redemption for which he came.

So, the first distraction would have been to get sweet revenge on his enemies and those who refused to believe in him. The second distraction, verse 54, would have been a derailment of the mission by power-hungry advisers that surrounded him – especially if he didn't have a mind of his own and if he was not totally committed to obeying the instructions of God.

Verse 54

"Lord do you want us to call fire down from heaven to destroy them?"

(Luke 9:54)

The disciples, of course, were familiar with the story of Elijah, how he called fire on the messengers of King Ahaziah (you can read it 2 Kings 1.) They knew the biography of Elijah the Tishbite and how he dealt with godless unbelievers in Samaria, thousands of years gone by. "Now Lord," they said, "the Samaritans are at it again, committing the same act of unbelief. Elijah destroyed their forefathers. You should do likewise – after all, some of the people think you are Elijah that has come back to life!"

Well, if Yeshua had followed their counsel, it would have been a complete distraction to his mission; an unnecessary courting of attention to himself. If He, the Redeemer and Saviour of the world, started to destroy people by fire, He would have contradicted himself. The disciples, in search of power and the spectacular, had forgotten that he had told them the devil has come to steal, kill and destroy, but He had come to give life and give life more abundantly. Destroying the Samaritans would have attracted bad publicity—as you know, bad news travels farther than good news.

I once heard a radio discussion between the Archbishop of Canterbury, a Chief Rabbi and one of the Imams in the UK. They were discussing about peace; how all the religions could live in harmony with each other. Did this attract a lot of media coverage? No! Not even the BBC. It had limited coverage. Why? Because peaceful and cordial meetings do not make good journalism (reading).

However, if it was bad news, it would make the evening news and be published on the front pages of the dailies. That was the world then and that is how it is even till today. The Lord did not want to give in to the world system. His ways are far away removed from ours.

Find out what your mission and calling is in God. Let no one distract you, let no one deceive you and let no one derail you. They may even say that you've got no power, no anointing like Elijah – do not go rushing in to show them how powerful you are. Do not go seeking for the power of Beelzebub. If you do, you will not recover. The power of Beelzebub is so visible – a "razzmatazz" for all to see; but the power of God, though not always visible, is still mighty to the pulling down of any stronghold. Their question was "Lord, do you want us to make a show of them? Should we make a show out of them?"

Read verse 55

"I am focused and committed to obeying the instructions of My Father, even if it looks foolish to you. Even if I look weak to you." The rest of the passage from verses 57-62 teaches us about the "wannabe followers of the Lord Yeshua."

Many of us are "wannabe followers" of Christ. What the Lord said to them then, He is saying to us today. "Be focused and committed to the Word—laws and instructions of God—even if doing so makes you look stupid, weak, gullible and of no reputation; even if doing so makes you lose family and friends.

The first one said "I will follow you wherever you go."

The Lord knows us better than we know ourselves. What do you seek when you come to God? Is it fame, fortune and lots of luxury? Yeshua said to this seeker, "Sorry, it is not about luxury and comfort. If you want to follow me, be focused and committed even when it is not as glamorous or luxurious as you would like."

Verses 59-60 shows us the awesome comparative severity of our calling. Our calling is not a joke, and if we understand it properly, everything else fades into insignificance when compared to the commission to preach and proclaim the kingdom of God. "If I say follow me," the Lord was saying, "just follow me, no excuses; even in situations as severe as foregoing the burying of a loved one." The last one of the "wannabe" followers was giving the Lord some conditions.

What condition are you giving the Lord, dear reader? What are you waiting for before you start taking His words seriously? Can anyone hold Him to ransom and say, "unless you do this first, unless I finish with my exams, unless I first buy a house, I am too young, unless I've sinned enough, I am too old, unless you show me some fire works from heaven... I haven't said that I will not follow you, just give me time to say goodbye to my old ways, old friends and old habits – give me time."

The Lord says be focused on and committed to me now, don't wait for tomorrow because you haven't got tomorrow in the bag. The question is: what should be your determination today?

Child of God, what have you learnt from this study? Would you make a rededication or recommitment to the Lord Yeshua the Messiah today? He is saying, "Come, and follow me." Would you say, "Yes, Lord." Or would you say, "Back off. Hold on a bit..." or would you be committed today in blind obedience to His Word? May the Lord bless you and give you strength today, as you give yourself wholeheartedly to Him. Amen.

Luke Chapter 10

3

LABOURERS OF THE KINGDOM: TEN THINGS TO BEAR IN MIND

Luke 10:1-16

Have you ever heard people—believers and unbelievers alike—complain and moan about the proliferation of churches? They say that churches are everywhere. "Look at Nigeria, for instance, there is a church on every street corner! They are springing up like mushrooms. No, not me, I am not going to any of those mushroom churches!"

To the people complaining, the above phenomenon is a bad and dubious thing, a thing to be really careful of. But from the text we are about to look at, we will hear the Lord Yeshua say: "There's a lot of work to be done. I've sent out some people before but even now I am going to send out some more." He compared the work of salvation and redemption to a farmer's business. That's why the key verse of our study in this segment is Luke 10:2. "The harvest truly is great, but the labourers are few; pray ye therefore the Lord of the harvest, that he would send labourers into His harvest."

This is why I want to share with you – as we continue in our study of Luke - "Ten Things To Bear In Mind As Labourers Of The Kingdom."

It is taken from Luke 10:1-16

> [1]After these things the Lord appointed seventy others also, and sent them two by two before His face into every city and place where He Himself was about to go. [2]Then He said to them, "The harvest truly is great, but the laborers are few; therefore pray the Lord of the harvest to send out laborers into His harvest. [3]Go your way; behold, I send you out as lambs among wolves. [4]Carry neither money bag, knapsack, nor sandals; and greet no one along the road. [5]But whatever house you enter, first say, 'Peace to this house.' [6]And if a son of peace is there, your peace will rest on it; if not, it will return to you. [7]And remain in the same house, eating and drinking such things as they give, for the laborer is worthy of his wages. Do not go from house to house. [8]Whatever city you enter, and they receive you, eat such things as are set before you. [9]And heal the sick there, and say to them, 'The kingdom of God has come near to you.' [10]But whatever city you enter, and they do not receive you, go out into its streets and say, [11]'The very dust of your city which clings to us we wipe off against you. Nevertheless

know this, that the kingdom of God has come near you.' ¹²But I say to you that it will be more tolerable in that Day for Sodom than for that city.

¹³"Woe to you, Chorazin! Woe to you, Bethsaida! For if the mighty works which were done in you had been done in Tyre and Sidon, they would have repented long ago, sitting in sackcloth and ashes. ¹⁴But it will be more tolerable for Tyre and Sidon at the judgment than for you. ¹⁵And you, Capernaum, who are exalted to heaven, will be brought down to Hades. ¹⁶He who hears you hears Me, he who rejects you rejects Me, and he who rejects Me rejects Him who sent Me."

(Luke 10:1-16)

The Lord likened the believers' life to that of a farmer. A farmer's job is to sow and harvest. He does that all year round. As long as the earth remains, there will always be seedtime and harvest time, all-year round. So, those who complain that there are too many churches or ministries springing up need to see the issue from this perspective.

When a believer complains without putting this into consideration, he reveals a lack of understanding of what the kingdom of heaven is all about; he does not know what the Saviour has come to do. Such a believer is selfishly saying, "I am saved, and that settles it. That's enough. You keep saving more people, and there will be no room for all of us in the end." They become like the prophet Jonah, they'd rather run away to Joppa than preach to save the perishing souls around them.

That's the mind of those who see things in the flesh. But the one who knows everyone and sees everything in the Spirit saw the period we live in today and said 2000 years ago that the harvest is truly great, massive and overwhelming. He asked us to pray because we are going to need more believers, more workers. As for the unbelievers who complain about churches here and there and everywhere -what do you expect?

They are still in the camp of the enemy. The enemy wants them to believe that there's no need for more believers hence, no need for more churches hence, no need for more workers. Thank God that out of those in the world who hold such views, God is still graciously saving many from the kingdom of darkness into His Kingdom of light. My sisters and brothers, please let us not buy into the lies and deceit of the devil.

By relaxing, taking things coolly and saying, "The harvesting of souls is not that urgent or important. Let's leave it for later. We don't need more workers, we can manage; it's not that huge." Let's not be short-sighted. Yeshua, the Saviour himself has said that the harvest is huge; let's not call him a liar.

Have you got relatives and friends? Have you got brothers and sisters? Have they come into the kingdom of God? Where will they spend eternity if you don't do everything possible to bring them to God? That's what our study today is all about: The harvest is truly huge and humongous, and they have to be gathered into the Kingdom.

Let's go back to our text Luke 10:1-16.

Verses 1-2

We know from all our studies so far in Luke that the Lord had a huge following; His regular apostles and disciples notwithstanding. He even had secret disciples who believed in him – hence they were believers nevertheless. We know of Nicodemus who come to Him at night. We also know Joseph of Arimathea who took responsibility for the burial of the Lord's body, and many other secret disciples like that. In the previous chapter, we read of a group of people who were going around doing miracles, signs and wonders in the Lord's name. They were not the regular disciples that the crowd knew, but they were doing the job because they believed in Yeshua the Messiah, and were using his name to do His work.

The disciples wanted to stop them. "How many more disciples are you going to have, besides us?" they wondered. Who knows how many more secret disciples there were out there at the time. So, you see why there will never be enough. He appointed another seventy and sent them out into the field. The Bible says He appointed them. What about you; He has also appointed you. Christ's appointment is not just for pastors and ministers. No, the message here is for all believers whether they are well-known or obscure. The seventy that Yeshua sent out were not even named. Wherever we are, the Lord is still sending people as labourers, soul gatherers. Listen carefully, you might hear your call – and when you do, please obey it.

Item No 1: Verses 1-2
We are labourers. The work is huge.
We need to pray and ask the Lord,
the owner of the harvest
to enlist more labourers into His work.

Item No 2: Verse 3
The road is fraught with danger.
The road is hard and rough.
Deceivers and seducers
Are out there with a manace
To hurt or take your head.
But go anyway, I am with you
Am I not the One sending you?
I will never leave you nor forsake you.

Item No 3: Verses 4-6
I will provide for you.
You will lack nothing.
Don't go in with money in mind;
don't go for riches, glamour, or fame;
don't be distracted by these things,
and don't be distracted by anyone.

Yeshua also told them, *Don't get into stop-and-greet ritual*. This bit of the instruction reminds me of the time I was growing up as a young boy in my village in Igboland. The culture was that you did not pass an elder without bowing gently to greet him or her. The Yoruba people would understand this passage more because whilst the Igbos would bow gently, the Yoruba boy would fall flat on his face to respect the elder he is greeting. The point was that the greetings were a kind of ritual that were performed and it did not matter how many elders we met on our way, we must do the same and show respect.

Can you imagine then if your mother sent you out for an urgent errand; perhaps to fetch a doctor because someone was sick? What will happen if you spent the rest of the evening stopping and greeting everyone you meet. Surely, you will not treat the errand with the urgency it deserves.

The Lord was being metaphorical, of course. He was not against greetings and salutations. All He was saying is that we should treat the spreading of His word with such seriousness, because there is nothing more important and there is no time to waste.

He said: Just take my peace and give my peace wherever you go. You have the authority to do so. You have my permission; you have my authority to bless peoples and their homes. To bless towns, cities and nations, to give them my peace and to take it back if they refuse it.

Item No 4: Verses 7-8

God is no respecter of persons. Do not be partial. Give respect to the rich as well as to the poor. Don't keep moving from place to place, favouring the big people and despising the small. Whatever you are given wherever you go, be grateful and thank God for it. Most importantly do the work for which I send you, even in such circumstances. You must heal the sick; and do not forget to tell them that all this is because the Kingdom of heaven has drawn near to them. In other words, "Come on board, that's why we are here."

Item No 5: Verses 7-10

You must realise that this good news of peace between God and man is for any time, any place and anywhere.

Go! Even at inconvenient hard times.
Go! Even if they receive you not.
Go! Even so when they receive you.
They may look different.
They may appear uninterested
They may even be antagonistic
Just present the Gospel.
Let God do the rest.

Item No 6: Verses 10-12

You cannot force people into the kingdom of safety. As long as you declare the benefits of the Kingdom and highlight the dangers of not accepting the kingdom of God, the rest of the work is God's to finish.

Remind them that the kingdom of God has come so near to them and that they'd be making a wrong decision if they reject God's offer of love and peace. You cannot force people. They must make up their own minds. They must take responsibility for their own soul.

Item No 7: Verses 10-11

Some will reject the good news, but do not take it personally.

Item No 8: Verses 8-13

Miracles signs and wonders are important. They are part and parcel of your calling. However, they are not the measure of the harvest, souls are. "I did some miracles in Chorazin," the Lord said. "I did some in Tyre and Sidon; but did they repent in ashes and rush into the kingdom of God? I did these things to show the power of God. Did they not see the power of God? Did they rush into the safety of God? No!"

Woe to the Chorazins of this world. Woe to the Tyre and Sidons; those who see the miracles of God by the bucket load and still do not accept His salvation, protection, rule and kingdom. Do not be fooled, my brother and sister; people may see all the miracles signs and wonders and still reject God. Yes, miracles, signs and wonders are important, but they are not the be-all-and-end-all of God's Kingdom. So what is, you may ask? Well, according to one songwriter, it is:

Item No 9: Verses 1-16
Righteousness, peace, joy in the Holy Ghost
Righteousness, peace and joy in the Holy Ghost
That's the kingdom of God
Don't you wanna be a part of the kingdom
Don't you wanna be a part of the kingdom
Come on - come on everybody.
© Helena Barrington

Item No 10: Verses 1-16
We have a linkage.
We have a lineage
When we're in line with the Kingdom.
We are in link with the Father.
We are his disciples.
We know that he has sent us
When we go as he sends us
We have a link with the Master
And he is our link to the Father.
"The world, I know, will reject you.
As they rejected Me.
And yet it did not stop me
From going to die for you.
So when the world would reject you
And pour their scorn on you.
Don't fail to wipe your tears on Me
Who is your link to God.
And never fight this war alone.
Return to barracks, plug into the link
Switch on to Me your current and your strength
Your Saviour and your Redeemer –
Yeshua, the Messiah, the Lord of the Harvest.
For the harvest is truly great
But the labourers are few.
God Bless You.

4

THE AUTHORITY IN THE WORD

Luke 10:17-42

Have you been in a class or training situation, lately? Have you had a trainer or facilitator who was new to you or the group? What does he or she do? Well, trainers will always start with a little chat (an icebreaker), and then get you to introduce yourselves. You may think they are being nice, but as a matter of fact, they are trying to know you by studying your responses. They want to get a picture of you, a first impression of what you know or don't know.

How do they accomplish this? By studying and analysing your first few words. From these they form an opinion of who you are or what they think you may know. There is power and authority in words, hence the need to revisit this topic in this section.

The Authority in the Word

Our text is still Luke 10:17-42. People will never know what you are capable of doing, what you are thinking in your mind, how you analyse information and carry out tasks, until they hear you. This is so because of the power in words, whether spoken or written.

I worked for over 20 years with people with learning disabilities. Some of the service users looked so well and healthy. They were handsome, beautiful and elegant. The only thing that lets some of them down is when they open their mouths to speak. Some, though adults, could not read or write. In situations like these, we come to appreciate the authority we possess through our spoken or written words.

In the Saturday school that I have run in England for many years, I have seen children from the same family exhibit different levels of articulation from each other. In some cases, the youngest is more articulate than the older ones. In situations like that, you can understand why the young boy seems to command respect not only from his older siblings, but from his father and mother also. There is power in the use of words. There is power in what you know but most especially in what you write and say.

Let us look at some Scripture verses to see the use of words and the power in how they are used.

> [17]Then the seventy returned with joy, saying, "Lord, even the demons are subject to us in Your name." [18]And He said to them, "I saw Satan fall like lightning from heaven. [19]Behold, I give you the authority to trample on serpents and scorpions, and over all the power of the enemy, and nothing shall by any

means hurt you. [20]Nevertheless do not rejoice in this, that the spirits are subject to you, but rather rejoice because your names are written in heaven."

(Luke 10:17-20)

Imagine what would have been the case if the seventy disciples returned to the Lord Yeshua, rejoined the crowd, and did not utter a word. First of all, the passage we are reading here would have been omitted completely. Secondly, no one, including you and I today, would have known how they felt, what they saw or what they did – except of course, Yeshua himself who knows and sees everything. Through their words we saw their emotions. Through words, we can see what they were rejoicing about and how the Lord responded to them. That is why I have captioned this section, *The power and authority in the Word*.

I could have said there is power and authority in *words*. But I said there is power and authority in THE WORD. The emphasis here is that there are *words* and there is *The Word*. If the ordinary words that ordinary people speak have an impact on peoples lives, how much more the Word? The Bible says: In the beginning was the Word and the Word was with God and the Word was God – the Word was Jesus – Yeshua the Messiah – nothing was created or made except through Him, the Word. So the seventy disciples shared the Word and they saw the power and authority in the Word.

In verses 19-20, we see the Lord Yeshua as He confers on His disciples more power and authority by using words. He spoke it out and into their spirits. Do you know that you've got the power and authority given to you to speak life into people – to give them better life here on earth and to give them eternal life in the life to come? But to do that or to be the Word, you've got to let the Word of God, Yeshua the Messiah himself, dwell in you richly. Then whatever you say or whoever you bless will be blessed indeed – because you carry Him, the Word, in the inside of you.

The power and authority in the Word started with Yeshua saying something, his disciples hearing it and believing it. His disciples then acted on them and saw the power and authority in the Word.

Their experience is an example for us, showing that if we hear the Word, believe in and act on it, we will see tremendous changes in our lives and the lives of people around us.

In this passage, we also see the importance of a master, leader, parent or an elder giving their consent and their blessing. We must never underestimate the importance of this.

The disciples had obeyed their Master and were now reporting back to Him. And because they carried out his instructions, He spoke more blessings over them.

How do you feel about words today? The words that people speak to you and the words you speak to others? What about the words that God speaks to you, or the one you are reading now? What will you do with them? There is power and authority in the Word.

I remember back in the late 1970s and the early 80s in Nigeria, when even unbelievers liked to talk to believers so that the believers can talk to them and bless them. They believed and received the blessings that the believers gave. How did that happen? Well in those days, believers hardly said "Good morning, good afternoon, thank you very much." No, they said 'Praise the Lord' and 'God bless you'. These were their watch-words and greetings.

A story was told of an unbelieving woman who later became a believer. How was she converted? As the story goes, she was a street trader who, most of the time, did not see a lot happening in her business. However, a particular young Christian man will usually pass by and say "God bless you ma'am." The woman would say, "Thank you." Over time, she observed that whenever the man passed and greeted her, she would have a bumper sale and a wonderful day. In essence, she recognised the power and authority in the spoken word. She now made sure that she saw the young man every morning in order to hear "God bless you."

What an enormous power we believers have in the Word of God; power to bless the world and be a blessing! Try it. You will be a great blessing rather than a curse. Try saying to people you meet, "God bless you," "God will provide for you," "God loves you," "God will sort it out for you." These words of encouragement will help your friends and relatives more than any chit chat or advice you can give them in times of trouble.

This is how that woman later turned to God and became a believer. God bless you as you listen. God bless you as you put it into practice in Yeshua's name – Amen.

> [21]In that hour Jesus rejoiced in spirit, and said, I thank thee, O Father, Lord of heaven and earth, that thou hast hid these things from the wise and prudent, and hast revealed them unto babes: even so, Father; for so it seemed good in thy sight. [22]All things are delivered to me of my Father: and no man knoweth who the Son is, but the Father; and who the Father is, but the Son, and he to whom the Son will reveal him. [23]And he turned him unto his disciples, and said privately, Blessed are the eyes which see the things that ye see: [24]For I tell you, that many prophets and kings have desired to see those things which ye see, and have not seen them; and to hear those things which ye hear, and have not heard them. [25]And, behold, a certain lawyer stood up, and tempted him, saying, Master, what shall I do to inherit eternal life? [26]He said unto him, What is written in the law? how readest thou? [27]And he answering said, Thou shalt love the Lord thy God with all thy heart, and with all thy soul, and with all thy strength, and with all thy mind; and thy neighbour as thyself. [28]And he said unto him, Thou hast answered

right: this do, and thou shalt live. ²⁹But he, willing to justify himself, said unto Jesus, And who is my neighbour?

(Luke 10:21-29)

Verses 21-24

Unless people speak, you will never fully understand their thoughts and behaviour. Until the Lord Yeshua responded we could never have known how He felt about their return (how happy he was). Until He responded, we would never have known that He had read their minds and can see that they were preoccupied with, at that time, who's going to be on the left and on his right in the kingdom. Until people speak, you can never know whether they are the emotional type, the scary type, the envious and jealous type. You will take them like every other human being. Until they speak, you cannot classify them.

For example, if you buy a car or a house, you would want to show it to friends and well-wishers. But if one of the people you are showing shows no sign of rejoicing with you and says: "People have been buying houses since time immemorial; so what's so special about this one?" Even if he says it smiling, you will feel the power in his words and become cautious as to what you say to him.

Also, when you say words that are not encouraging or uplifting to people, words that are hurtful, you don't know how much destructive power you have unleashed through your words—certainly not the power of God. And if you are not unleashing

God's power, you will be unleashing the power of the enemy. You will become the disciple of the devil rather than the disciple of Yeshua. May that not be your portion. Amen.

The Lord made them know, in no uncertain terms, that what they were seeing and experiencing was "classified information"; that it was a privilege for them to be experiencing what they were experiencing.

Verses 25-29

This is the story of a learned gentleman, a lawyer. He came to tempt the Lord Yeshua; he wanted to embarrass Him with high legal and deep philosophical questions. Our learned gentleman was determined to make Him feel ashamed for claiming to be a teacher, not to talk of being the Messiah of the Jews.

Imagine if he had stayed in the crowd, listened to everything and never said a word. We would not have known what a smart-aleck he really was. As soon as he opened his mouth, not only did Yeshua the Messiah, know what he was trying to do, His disciples also became aware. Even though the Word had been written down somewhere else in Scripture, the Lord had to answer him with spoken words, so that there and then he felt the power in the spoken word – spoken with the authority of the Word Himself.

Next reading, verses 30-37.

> [30]And Jesus answering said, A certain man went down from Jerusalem to Jericho, and fell among thieves, which stripped him of his raiment, and wounded him, and departed,

leaving him half dead. ³¹And by chance there came down a certain priest that way: and when he saw him, he passed by on the other side. ³²And likewise a Levite, when he was at the place, came and looked on him, and passed by on the other side. ³³But a certain Samaritan, as he journeyed, came where he was: and when he saw him, he had compassion on him, ³⁴And went to him, and bound up his wounds, pouring in oil and wine, and set him on his own beast, and brought him to an inn, and took care of him. ³⁵And on the morrow when he departed, he took out two pence, and gave them to the host, and said unto him, Take care of him; and whatsoever thou spendest more, when I come again, I will repay thee. ³⁶Which now of these three, thinkest thou, was neighbour unto him that fell among the thieves? ³⁷And he said, He that shewed mercy on him. Then said Jesus unto him, Go, and do thou likewise.

(Luke 10:30-37)

This section tells us of different people who saw the victim, had good thoughts in their minds but said or did nothing to the victim. They may even have had bad thoughts but did not dare to voice it out. Something in the line of: "All these Samaritan gangs! I wonder what he was doing around here? I wonder why they lynched him. You know how they are, these Samaritans, what they can get up to. I don't want to get involved. He may even be a drug pusher." Like some would say even here in UK. "All these Jamaican boys, all these Nigerian girls, you know how they behave, I don't even want to say a word. I don't want to know! Period."

But see the power loaded inside encouraging words, from the most unlikely person. The Samaritan man must, of course, have spoken to the Jewish victim to know that he was alive. He must have spoken to him while bandaging him. He spoke to the inn keepers. They saw his compassion through his words. There was so much power and authority in the Samaritan's words.

The inn-keepers said to themselves, "Well, see how much he has spent already on a stranger, a victim on the road. His word must be his bond. He will certainly keep his promise. Bring the victim in and let us care for him because of this man's word."

There is enormous power and authority in your word, my brother and sister! How much do people believe in what you say? Can people say of you, "Well, if that's what she says, that's ok, she will do it."? Or will they laugh and say, "Oh my word, who said that, James? And you believed him – well you must be so gullible. Don't you know James? When he says come, you better run for your life! If he says he's in Peckham and he's going to be 30 minutes, don't you believe a word of it. He's probably somewhere in Hackney!"

Can you imagine how awful that is? But there can be power in your words.

Let's hear the Lord Yeshua really emphasise what I've been talking about.

> [38] Now it came to pass, as they went, that he entered into a certain village: and a certain woman named Martha received him into her house. [39] And she had a sister called Mary, which also sat at Jesus' feet, and heard his word. [40] But Martha was cumbered about much serving, and came to him, and said, Lord, dost thou not care that my sister hath left me to serve alone? bid her therefore that she help me.
>
> [41] And Jesus answered and said unto her, Martha, Martha, thou art careful and troubled about many things: [42] But one thing is needful: and Mary hath chosen that good part, which shall not be taken away from her.
>
> **(Luke 10:38-42)**

This is the story of Mary and Martha. In this story, we see two women who both adored the Lord. Each one did what she thought was the best way to please the Lord at the time. From an African traditional point of view, we should be rooting for Martha, because she did the most important thing to do if a guest—a celebrity for that matter—came to her house; she provided hospitality. But the Lord said hospitality is fine but it is not the priority as far as God is concerned; hearing His word is of greater importance. It contains correction, instructions, directions, affection, compassion, to lead you in life. It even teaches on how to provide hospitality!

Verses 41-42

"Martha, Martha, you are worried and bothered about so many things, but only a few things are necessary. As a matter of fact, only one thing really matters: **the WORD**. It has exceeding power and authority. So you see, Mary has chosen the good part. The good part is the word of God, and no one has the power to take it away from her. So Martha, sit down at my feet and learn wisdom, hearken to my word and learn understanding." Surely, "wisdom is the principal thing."

Dearly beloved, what is the Lord saying to you and I today?

> [7]Wisdom is the principal thing; therefore get wisdom. And in all your getting, get understanding. [8]Exalt her, and she will promote you; She will bring you honor, when you embrace her. [9]She will place on your head an ornament of grace; a crown of glory she will deliver to you." [10]Hear, my son, and receive my sayings, and the years of your life will be many.
>
> **(Proverbs 4:7-10)**

The Lord bless and keep you
As you hear His words of instruction
Believe them and do them
And receive his blessings that
Makes rich and adds no sorrow to it.
Amen.

Luke Chapter 11

5

TEACH US TO PRAY

Luke 11:1-13

In this segment we will explore the subject of prayer. First of all, what is prayer? Payer is an appeal addressed to one's God. It can be in the form of thanks, appreciation or praise. It can also be an earnest request.

Prayers are made with words. But sometimes, they are expressed as thoughts in the mind. Whichever way you choose, the key factor is that prayer is directed to one's God.

So to pray, one must be able to believe in a god, or have a god who he believes is capable of hearing prayers; a god who is able to feel for them, hear their appeal or petition, and do something about it.

I believe also that for someone to believe in a god, he or she must believe in the capability of that god to do something about the situation he or she is bringing to that god. Believing in a god is believing in something or someone outside of oneself that is greater and more powerful. Even those who take their god to be the wooden elephant on the mantelpiece believe that this "god," though unable to move or speak, is able to hear them and do something about their petition. They also believe that their god is capable of sorting out things that they are not able to do.

Well, Christians also pray and we direct our prayers to the Almighty God.

As Christians, we believe:

- Our God is alive and is everywhere.
- God is capable of doing anything He chooses without restriction. He is in charge, in control and does not seek permission from any other authority or from His creation.
- God has feelings of love and compassion for his creation.
- God can hear us anytime and anywhere. He is capable of seeing and hearing of our situations all at once.

There is no "engaged tone" on God's line. There are no charges for "voicemail," be it leaving or receiving one. His line is wide open to all. Why? Because He wants His children and all His creation to communicate and interact with Him. He has made us and the whole universe as one giant "interactive computer." This inter-activeness is the main purpose of His creation. Otherwise, what use are we to a holy and contented God? From this understanding, we can see why people of old realised the importance of earnest, interactive conversation with God.

Before we proceed, let us read from Luke:

Teach Us to Pray

¹Now it came to pass, as He was praying in a certain place, when He ceased, that one of His disciples said to Him, "Lord, teach us to pray, as John also taught his disciples." ²So He said to them, "When you pray, say: Our Father in heaven, Hallowed be Your name. Your kingdom come Your will be done on earth as it is in heaven. ³Give us day by day our daily bread. ⁴And forgive us our sins, For we also forgive everyone who is indebted to us. And do not lead us into temptation, But deliver us from the evil one." ⁵And He said to them, "Which of you shall have a friend, and go to him at midnight and say to him, 'Friend, lend me three loaves; ⁶for a friend of mine has come to me on his journey, and I have nothing to set before him'; ⁷and he will answer from within and say, 'Do not trouble me; the door is now shut, and my children are with me in bed; I cannot rise and give to you'? ⁸I say to you, though he will not rise and give to him because he is his friend, yet because of his persistence he will rise and give him as many as he needs. ⁹"So I say to you, ask, and it will be given to you; seek, and you will find; knock, and it will be opened to you. ¹⁰For everyone who asks receives, and he who seeks finds, and to him who knocks it will be opened. ¹¹If a son asks for bread from any father among you, will he give him a stone? Or if he asks for a fish, will he give him a serpent instead of a fish? ¹²Or if he asks for an egg, will he offer him a scorpion? ¹³If you then, being evil, know

how to give good gifts to your children, how much more will your heavenly Father give the Holy Spirit to those who ask Him!"

(Luke 11:1-13)

Teach us to pray:

Verse 1: "Lord teach us to pray."
- The implication of this statement is that the disciples saw the need for prayer; they saw the importance of it.
- They realised that even though they have been following the Lord and watching him pray, they themselves did not pray.
- Even when they prayed, compared to the prayers of their Master, they certainly needed to learn how to pray properly and effectively.
- Though they were Jews, brought up in God-fearing families, where heads of families led in prayer, they had never witnessed the kind of answers to prayer that Yeshua had.

So, the disciples went to their Rabbi, Yeshua the Messiah, and asked Him to teach them how to pray.

In Bible times; great teachers gathered around themselves students or disciples, who learnt from them. Whatever the master taught the disciples was what they shaped their lives by. The same goes for every field of endeavour today, be it medicine, commerce or engineering. Students seek out places where they can learn the discipline they intend to live by.

People travelled thousands of miles to beg a great teacher or talent (like the Rabbi) to take them under his wings. Once the master accepts, they, with much joy, abandon everything else, including family and friends to follow their new-found way. There may be many "ways", but for them, they have found "their way." Hence, whatever their master says becomes great maxims that guide the students.

No wonder the disciples of Yeshua said, "Lord, teach us to pray. We have seen people pray at home. We have seen people pray in the synagogue. We have even prayed ourselves at different times. In contrast, we have also seen and heard you pray; we have heard you criticise some folks who did not pray aright. So please Lord, teach us how to pray *aright*." Knowing how much respect the Lord had for John the Baptist, the disciples reasoned that if prayer was good enough for John's disciples, it was also good for them.

Dearly beloved, if the disciples of Yeshua viewed prayer as an integral part of their lives, how much more you and I today? Maybe you already know how to pray. Like the disciples in this story, we need to know the *real* way of prayer from the Master himself.

Let us examine this portion of scripture to see what we can learn from the Lord Yeshua about prayer. Surely, if anyone should know how to interact with God, He should know.

Verse 2

Our Father which art in heaven, Hallowed be thy name.

The Lord Yeshua taught that when you pray, say "Our Father". In other words, when you pray, don't be thinking of Him only as God; approach him as your Father. But don't get too familiar that you lose respect for Him. Don't forget His name is holy; His name is to be honoured and revered. His name is hallowed, so don't call his name in vain or in disrespect.

Many have the notion that this was a prayer given by the Lord for us to recite. Surely, it is more than this; it is a framework or a template to guide individual prayer.

Verse 2

Thy kingdom come. Thy will be done, as in heaven, so in earth.

Saying 'thy kingdom come" always when we pray does not mean much to God unless we understand what we are saying. The Lord Yeshua wanted his disciples to know that prayer that pleases God is the one that acknowledges the rule of God in our lives; it is prayer that confesses that we will not do anything contrary to the King's decree. God, our Father, is the King of all kings. He rules in heaven and is obeyed in heaven. What the Lord was saying to His disciples was that God also needs to be obeyed and listened to on earth as well, as is the case in heaven. In other words, may His heavenly kingdom be established on earth.

Verse 3

Give us day by day our daily bread.

You can see what the Lord is saying here; that "it is no good just saying it." He wants us to know and believe it, that our father is Jehovah Jireh, the Great Provider, who is able to provide for and sustain us daily in His kingdom.

Verse 4
And forgive us our sins, for we also forgive everyone that is indebted to us.

This is a good example to prove that this prayer outline was not meant to be recited. It is a framework of things we need to take seriously as we pray; issues we need to have sorted out before approaching God. These include forgiveness of offences, issues of the heart that we may have against other people.

And lead us not into temptation.

Here we are taught to ask God for help whenever we pray; help that will keep us from falling. The Bible says, *"Let he that thinks he stands beware lest he falls"* (1 Corinthians 10:12). It is easy to feel complacent, relax our guards and not pray. When we do this, we are no longer relying on God for everything. When temptation comes, it will be easy to fall, no matter who we think we are in the Lord – Apostle, prophet or disciple.

Yielding to temptation, of course, means disobedience to God, and the Lord Yeshua warns us against disobeying God. He knows how much it will hurt our interactive relationship with God. Yeshua the Messiah, therefore, was saying to his disciples: Pray to God, weighing up what you say to Him and as you do, use this framework...

- Don't be a stranger, talk to God as a father.
- Don't get too familiar and forget that God is a holy God.
- Praise and worship Him as you mention His name.
- Don't forget that God is King. There is no other God or King in His kingdom. He is the first and the last; what He says goes, and there can be no argument.
- When you pray, believe in His ability to hear and act. Have faith in Him to provide. Even the most basic things like providing your daily bread."
- "You are all a bunch of sinners. Yes, you are saved only by grace. I forgave you your sins and thus you got saved. Before you approach me, forgive those who have wronged you just as I have forgiven you."
- The final point of his teaching was for us not to think we can stand without him. Don't you ever think you are a stronger Christian than anybody else.

You need God, even just to stand and be a Christian, hence the need for a regular, interactive relationship. In other words, whenever we pray, we must ask God to direct us in the way of righteousness, so that we can always be in right standing with him.

Verses 5-8

The rest of the passage is a warning and teaching about giving up. "I've prayed this prayer several times, nothing is happening, perhaps God is not listening, perhaps he's not interested in me." Well, the commandment from Yeshua the Messiah is, "thou shalt not give up, God is on the throne and in control. Be persistent."

Verses 9-10

Ask: Speak out your request. It is good to think or meditate on your prayers but God likes it too when you speak it out. When you voice out your prayers, not only does God hear them, people hear them and the devil also hears. It gives great honour and glory to God when He grants your request; it becomes a testimony for others to learn from and put their trust in God, and a great shame to the devil.

Seek: Seek the face of God for the solution to your problems. This injunction makes us realise that God is not our stooge or puppet who does what we want, when we want it. That's why he made Himself invisible and not commonly available. We therefore need to look for Him in a committed fashion.

Knock: As if seeking were not enough, we are encouraged to knock and rattle the gates of heaven. Show your desperation only to God. It is not that God is deaf, uncaring or unable to deal with your situation. Only don't be impatient as to give up. He wants to know whether you trust Him or not; whether you are going to quickly look for other solutions besides

Him. Don't forget, "He is God and there is no other." (Isaiah 45:22).

Watch out for his response.
It could be a 'No, not for you.'
It could be a 'not yet', later on
It could be, 'yeah, right now'.

Whatever is the case, He answers to every prayer. And may He answer your prayers today, for the Lord Yeshua's sake. Amen.

Verses 11-13

The Lord was teaching us in this passage to know that we have more of a Father in God than we have in our earthly fathers. Yet we seem to cleave to earthly fathers for our needs more than we cleave to God. The Lord was teaching that the reverse should be the case. It is true that in most cases, our earthly fathers love us, even though they are full of sin and can lack compassion sometimes. But they are nowhere near the grace, mercy and love that God has for us. God is prepared to give the Holy Spirit to help us creatively work and prosper in everything we do.

6

WHAT MORE DO YOU WANT?

Luke 11:14-36

Sometimes, I wonder about the multitude that followed Jesus around in the days of His ministry. I wonder whether some of them had anything else to do other than assemble wherever a crowd was gathering. Did they have jobs to go to? Did they have any deadlines to meet (especially when the teachings sometimes went on till late)? Did they have families—wives and children—to look after? Why did they spend so much time following Him everywhere, even the hard, unbelieving ones who made a nuisance of themselves whenever they spoke to him.

Well, the passage we are going to read proves that human beings have not changed much, even from the time of Yeshua, the Messiah. People still have deep longings and yearnings. They still chase after the spectacular. People are still searching for wisdom and understanding of the deeper meanings of life. People still need solutions to their many problems.

Some of the issues that people deal with are physical (seen), while others are metaphysical (unseen). So, when someone claims to have an answer to life's questions, people rush to see what is on offer. Who knows, this person could really possess the much-needed solution.

So, from the crowd that stand outside in the cold to see who is going to be evicted from their favourite reality show, to those who flock Christian events looking for answers to their prayers, people are still the same. Some, of course, just want to witness what is happening and have a good laugh.

Further to the fact above, is that humans are not easily pleased and satisfied. None of the solutions that prophets, teachers or wise men have offered has completely pleased man – not even that of Yeshua, the Messiah. No wonder why he exclaimed in the passage we are about to study, "What more do you want?"

In other words, "I have preached all day and done all these signs, but you are still not satisfied. I have cast out demons and healed many diseases; I even providing food for you to eat, and you are still not satisfied. *What more do you want? How else can I prove my love for you? What more proof do you need to believe in me? I gave you signs and you are still seeking for a sign. What more do you want?*"

Let's have a look at Luke 11:14-36.

> [14]And He was casting out a demon, and it was mute. So it was, when the demon had gone out, that the mute spoke; and the multitudes marveled. [15]But some of them said, "He casts

out demons by Beelzebub, the ruler of the demons." ¹⁶Others, testing Him, sought from Him a sign from heaven. ¹⁷But He, knowing their thoughts, said to them: "Every kingdom divided against itself is brought to desolation, and a house divided against a house falls. ¹⁸If Satan also is divided against himself, how will his kingdom stand? Because you say I cast out demons by Beelzebub. ¹⁹And if I cast out demons by Beelzebub, by whom do your sons cast them out? Therefore they will be your judges. ²⁰But if I cast out demons with the finger of God, surely the kingdom of God has come upon you. ²¹When a strong man, fully armed, guards his own palace, his goods are in peace. ²²But when a stronger than he comes upon him and overcomes him, he takes from him all his armor in which he trusted, and divides his spoils. ²³He who is not with Me is against Me, and he who does not gather with Me scatters.

²⁴"When an unclean spirit goes out of a man, he goes through dry places, seeking rest; and finding none, he says, 'I will return to my house from which I came.' ²⁵And when he comes, he finds it swept and put in order. ²⁶Then he goes and takes with him seven other spirits more wicked than himself, and they enter and dwell there; and the last state of that man is worse than the first."

²⁷And it happened, as He spoke these things, that a certain woman from the crowd raised her voice and said to Him, "Blessed is the womb that bore You, and the breasts which nursed You!" ²⁸But He said, "More than that, blessed are those who hear the word of God and keep it!"

²⁹And while the crowds were thickly gathered together, He began to say, "This is an evil generation. It seeks a sign, and no sign will be given to it except the sign of Jonah the prophet. ³⁰For as Jonah became a sign to the Ninevites, so also the Son of Man will be to this generation. ³¹The queen of the South will rise up in the judgment with the men of this generation and condemn them, for she came from the ends of the earth to hear the wisdom of Solomon; and indeed a greater than Solomon is here. ³²The men of Nineveh will rise up in the judgment with this generation and condemn it, for they repented at the preaching of Jonah; and indeed a greater than Jonah is here.

³³"No one, when he has lit a lamp, puts it in a secret place or under a basket, but on a lampstand, that those who come in may see the light. ³⁴The lamp of the body is the eye. Therefore, when your eye is good, your whole body also is full of light. But when your eye is bad, your body also is full of darkness.

³⁵Therefore take heed that the light which is in you is not darkness. ³⁶If then your whole body is full of light, having no part dark, the whole body will be full of light, as when the bright shining of a lamp gives you light."

(Luke 11:14-36)

In verses 14-16, you could hear the people teasing: "Yeah, yeah, yeah. You've done one from the devil; now do one from heaven." Miracles were now getting common and familiar. "Even worshippers of Beelzebub can heal the sick," they were saying. "Your first miracle was from Beelzebub, wasn't it? Now do one from heaven."

Fans always profess to know everything about their star, but most of the time they are wrong. These people thought that they knew what a miracle from Beelzebub looked like. They also believed they'd know when one from heaven is given. They demanded from Him a sign from heaven. *"Never mind this one; we want one from heaven."*

In today's society, many of us are no different. Some grade ministers by the miracles, signs and wonders they are able to perform. Even when a genuine miracle occurs, many will not recognise it because they are looking for something more spectacular – a sign "from heaven". Those who recognise the power of God, immediately start praising God; those who do not ask for more.

What more do you want?, Yeshua is asking. The people, in verses 15-16, were not ignorant. They knew the culture, history and legends. They knew the story of their forefathers' experiences on the way to the promised land. At one time, they ran out of food and were going to die if no one solved the food problem. "Come on, Moses, do something. You brought us out here. Did you bring us out here to kill us all?" They chided.

God did a miracle straight away from heaven.
Manna fell from heaven. Quail fell from heaven.
They had bread and they had meat from heaven.

They also knew the story of Elijah and the prophets of Baal. As far as they were concerned, Elijah did a miracle straight from heaven. Fire came down from heaven and consumed the sacrifice that Elijah set up on the alter.

They knew their history.
They knew their legends.
"Give us some food
Let's have some fire-works
Let's have a ball
Let's have a blast.", they cried.

They may be selective in their thinking but they will not forget the one about Noah preaching for many years, begging people to repent, turn around and follow God. They laughed him to scorn, especially whenever he mentioned that rain will fall and form a flood, the strength of which will sweep away the human race if they do not run into the ark and take refuge, and save their lives.

"Give us a sign.
Give us some food
Let's have a blast
Like fire-works from heaven."

"Silly unscientific old man. What do you know?
Even the most scientific ones among us
Have not discovered this thing you call rain.
You're being deluded. It will never happen."

They demanded for a sign. God gave them a sign. They all perished in the flood and didn't live to see the sights afterwards. Here, we see the same unbelief as people talked to the Lord Yeshua.

"Aye! Yeshua, you've done these ones –
We want one straight from heaven
Forget that one, that's Beelzebub stuff.
Let's see more, straight from heaven
Like Moses, Noah or Elijah stuff.
The teachers straight from heaven

The Lord replied to them, and I paraphrase.

"Let's get one thing straight here.
You are speaking way over your heads
You don't know what you are asking.
Yeah, I know you didn't say a word
But you were thinking those thoughts
I can read your minds, you know.

I know what you are thinking. You are saying. 'He is casting them out with the power of Beelzebub.'"

"Let me teach you one big principle that you have failed to realise."

Verses 17–20
A: Any kingdom divided against itself will fall. It would definitely not stand.
B: Mind what you are thinking or saying concerning the work of God. Accusations and dissentions will not get you anywhere.
C: Try and recognise the finger of God's visitation in your lifetime. Accept it, call on Him and you will be saved.

"If you accuse me of casting out demons with the power of Beelzebub, what powers are you and your children, who are steeped into idolatry casting them out with?"

Verses 21-22
"Let me tell you how it works. Let me tell you what's happening here. God is the One casting out demons and setting people free. For anyone to come into the house of a strongman and tie him up and hold him hostage in his own house, that someone must be stronger than the strongman. Otherwise that person could not do what he had done."

The Lord went on to explain to them that God is stronger than all their gods put together, including

Beelzebub. That's why He is able to walk into the dwelling place of the evil spirits and bind and cast them out without much resistance. He admonished them that all they needed to do was to accept and recognise that the power and glory, that is, the kingdom of God, had come in their midst, in their lifetime and all they needed was to praise God and be grateful.

Verse 23

The Lord advised them that there is no room for sitting on the fence. You are either in or out; there was no middle ground. You are either with Him or you are not. Those who are with Him are safe. Those who are not with Him are not.

Verses 24-26 teach us to be committed to the Lord. To avoid making our hearts a lodging place for the enemy. The Bible encourages us:

> "Guard your heart with all diligence; for out of it flows the issues of life. Put away from you a froward mouth and perverse lips, put far from you."

(Proverbs 4:23-24)

Verses 27-28

[27]While Jesus was saying these things, one of the women in the crowd raised her voice and said to Him, "Blessed is the womb that bore You and the breasts at which You nursed." [28]But He

said, "On the contrary, blessed are those who hear the word of God and observe it."

(Luke 11:27,28 NASB)

The woman in the story above, humanly speaking, was right. She said what majority of the mothers and fathers in the crowd were thinking but never voiced it out. Is there anyone of us who would not like to be a close family member of this miracle working, power motivator Messiah? We would not even mind being a distant relative!

The woman wished it was her own son that everyone was crowding around to listen to; and since he was not hers, she simply expressed how proud the mother of the Lord Yeshua must be.

You would have thought that the Lord would receive such an accolade with joy. But he did not. Instead, he responded in a way that would have shocked his hearers and perhaps left a big "Selah" in their hearts. He made them realise that He was not there to teach humanistic ways of thinking and doing things; He was there to teach the righteousness of God—heaven's way of doing things. He was there to teach what was more important to God.

Therefore, it did not matter who their mother or their father was—whether they be bishops archbishops, famous and prominent in the church, Jew or Gentile. It did not matter who nursed or nurtured them. It did not matter what their background was; what mattered was their relationship with God and how seriously they took His word.

Verses 29-30

Some of them were still demanding a sign. He said (my paraphrase):

"You want a sign? I'll give you another sign.

You remember Jonah? That's the kind of sign you need with your rebellion and unbelief. To be swallowed up by a big fish until you show some sign of repentance."

Verse 31

"You want a sign? I'll give you a sign. But you wouldn't recognise one if it hit you on the face. You lack vision, you lack wisdom. The Queen of Sheba heard about the wisdom of God through Solomon and came all the way from the East to listen and pay homage, while people in Jerusalem at the time took it for granted "

Verse 32

"Talking about signs and wonders, the signs of Jonah and the people of Nineveh; at least the people of Nineveh repented and were forgiven. They heard the good news that there was a chance they could be saved if they turned around from doing their own things and obeyed God. They listened, repented and were saved. But you lot seem to want to die in your sins."

Verses 32-34

"I am come as light but you prefer darkness. You prefer things hidden rather than things exposed in the open. You like things done behind closed doors with the sons of Beelzebub rather than in the light and with the finger of God. *What more do you want? What haven't I done for you? Why can't you see the light? Why can't you listen to me and live?"*

Verses 35–36

We are being taught here by the Lord, that we have two sides to us, as human beings, the dark side and the light side. It is obvious that the dark side is evil while the light side is not. We also know that the dark side relates to the influences and powers of the evil one, the devil. There is no doubt therefore that the light side comes from the influences of the Living God Himself.

We learn also from the two verses above that one influence has the ability to overshadow and cover the other. In other words, darkness has the potential to cover light and light has the potential to wipe out darkness completely.

It is also clear from that passage that the ability for any of the influences to overpower the other is dependent on us human beings who stand in the middle as receptacles. We have the ability to receive or reject the influences as they try to affect us. Whatever the influence, we have the inbuilt capacity, the freewill to say yes or no.

The Lord, therefore, warns us to watch what we see and what we let into our soul. He warns us not to allow the light in us to be quenched by darkness, the evil one and the evil side.

Verse **36** seems to be saying that darkness can actually destroy the potential in us; while if we clear all the dark side through the words He speaks to us, we would be so illuminated that our good qualities and full potentials will shine out like the noon day sun.

We can still hear the Lord say:

'What more do you want?
What more can I do?
What more can I say?
The devil has come to kill
The devil has come to steal
But I have come to give life
The devil has come to destroy
I have come to give light and life
Abundant life, leading to eternal life.
Choose me now, Choose life forever'

Again, these two verses above serve as a warning to those ministers, those "Christians" who think they can have the Lord as well as the devil, all at the same time. They think it's their duty to explore and experiment with all kinds of philosophies and all kinds of spirits. They think they can eat their cake and still have it. In these two verses alone, we learn that you cannot eat your cake and have it.

The more you experiment with other philosophies, whether they be eastern or western, the more you will encounter spirits other than the Spirit of the Living God. The Lord is likely, then, to leave you to it, because He does not share His glory with anyone or anything. The result will be that the evil spirit will take over and the person's whole life will be full of darkness. The end of such a person will be death—eternal death.

7

OUTSIDE VERSUS INSIDE

Luke 11:37-54

Generally, we accept that everything that has an outside must have an inside. They go hand-in-hand, and one cannot do without the other. This principle applies to both animate and inanimate objects, including plants, animals and human beings.

It is also accepted in all cases, that what affects one affects the other, whether inside or outside. If, for instance, the inside of a plant is sick and rotting away, the whole of the outside will look sickly and out of sorts; the same goes for any animal whatsoever. The degree to which the sickness or the un-wellness on the inside surfaces on the outside is dependent on the type and gravity of un-healthiness.

Since humans are not just physical but also spiritual beings, this principle applies in the spiritual dimension as well.

The real inside of a person is not just the physical organs like the heart, liver, lungs, or the brain. The real person is in the soul and spirit, which is on the inside. And according to the principle we have posited earlier, whatever affects the inside of a person or thing, will automatically affect the outside of it. Spiritual entities will of course require spiritual sustenance to keep it strong and healthy while physical things will require physical nutrients to keep it going.

In the passage we are about to study (Luke 11:37-54), we see the Lord Yeshua reiterating to the Pharisees the importance of caring for their inside, their inner-self, as much as they care for their outside. He gave them a teaching that I have entitled **Outside Verses Inside**.

Let's read the story.

> [37]And as He spoke, a certain Pharisee asked Him to dine with him. So He went in and sat down to eat. [38]When the Pharisee saw it, he marveled that He had not first washed before dinner. [39]Then the Lord said to him, "Now you Pharisees make the outside of the cup and dish clean, but your inward part is full of greed and wickedness. [40]Foolish ones! Did not He who made the outside make the inside also? [41]But rather give alms of such things as you have; then indeed all things are clean to you. [42]"But woe to you Pharisees! For you tithe mint and rue and all manner of herbs, and pass by justice and the love of God. These you ought to have done, without leaving the others undone. [43]Woe to you Pharisees! For you love the best seats in the synagogues and greetings in the marketplaces. [44]Woe to you, scribes and Pharisees, hypocrites! For you are like graves which are not seen, and the men who walk over them are not aware of them."

⁴⁵Then one of the lawyers answered and said to Him, "Teacher, by saying these things You reproach us also." ⁴⁶And He said, "Woe to you also, lawyers! For you load men with burdens hard to bear, and you yourselves do not touch the burdens with one of your fingers. ⁴⁷Woe to you! For you build the tombs of the prophets, and your fathers killed them. ⁴⁸In fact, you bear witness that you approve the deeds of your fathers; for they indeed killed them, and you build their tombs. ⁴⁹Therefore the wisdom of God also said, 'I will send them prophets and apostles, and some of them they will kill and persecute,'⁵⁰that the blood of all the prophets which was shed from the foundation of the world may be required of this generation, ⁵¹from the blood of Abel to the blood of Zechariah who perished between the altar and the temple. Yes, I say to you, it shall be required of this generation. ⁵²"Woe to you lawyers! For you have taken away the key of knowledge. You did not enter in yourselves, and those who were entering in you hindered." ⁵³And as He said these things to them, the scribes and the Pharisees began to assail Him vehemently, and to cross-examine Him about many things, ⁵⁴lying in wait for Him, and seeking to catch Him in something He might say, that they might accuse Him.

(Luke 11:37-54)

Verses 37-38

During the Lord's earthly ministry, everyone wanted to get into His good book – including the Pharisees who did not believe in Him. They questioned everything He did and tried to find out if He really was who He said He was. They scrutinised everything He did or said. But that did not stop them from inviting Him for dinner, lunch or supper.

Some of the Pharisees and political leaders were being smart. They tried to play their cards right. They were not sure who Yeshua was but just in case He emerged to be who He claimed to be, they needed the benefit of his friendship.

That could be one reason why they invited him for meals. The other reason could be that some of the Pharisees, even though they disliked Him, wanted to be seen with this famous person; a kind of spin-doctoring; courting with fame by association. The more people talked about the Lord on that particular day, the more they mentioned the Pharisee at whose house He had dinner. Otherwise, why would the Pharisee throw a party for someone who is not normally on his friends list?

By inviting Yeshua for dinner, they thought He would not speak His mind or respond to the things they say. But every occasion is a teaching and training ground for the Lord. He used every opportunity to teach the Pharisees, the multitude that followed Him and His disciples. This particular occasion was an opportunity for Him to teach about "outside verses inside."

Normally, the Lord would give thanks before a meal but on this occasion He decided not to do so. And no sooner than He went in, reclined at the table and started eating, than the Pharisee showed his surprise. The Lord had not ceremonially washed His hands, feet, eyes, ears, mouth and nose before partaking of the meal! These, they believed, were parts of a person's body that could lead him to sin.

Straight away, the Lord rebuked the hypocrisy of the Pharisees. He said; "You Pharisees clean the outside of the cup and platter, but on the inside, you are full of robbery and wickedness" (verse 39). Washing the body ceremonially before eating, as well as the utensils was supposed to ensure that the people were clean and uncontaminated. But the Lord told them that what they were trying to wash away physically was already resident in their hearts.

Sometimes, people bend their necks and pray piously at every meal and function, but if they are still robbing each other in one way or the other, their prayers are being wasted. Ceremonial washing was symbolic of cleansing, a kind of baptism for the remission of sins. The Lord Yeshua, the Messiah, did not have any sin, so it didn't really concern Him. He didn't need the washing for what it represented.

Verses 40-41

Just as Yeshua took the opportunity to teach the Pharisees at the time, we also need to understand that if we are going to cleanse ourselves at all, we must start from the inside; which will then radiate and come out on the outside. God created the inside as well as the outside. We should look after both.

Verse 42 gives us some illustration of what outside verses inside could be. The Pharisees did some practical, physical and outward displays that let the world know how good they were. They paid their tithes, one tenth of their income, to the synagogue. They tithed on all kinds of garden herbs, including mint and rue. Some of these herbs had a sweet aroma that filled the room as they walked in with the tithe. Obviously, people would notice, praise and applaud them, with the Pharisees enjoying the acknowledgement and respect.

We notice that the Lord did not condemn their giving of tithes; rather, He said they should have given attention to the inside as well as the outside; they should not neglect one for the other. The "inside," He said, comprised of giving justice and love to our fellow men.

We also notice that the passage we are looking at has six "woes" in it. The word woe, of course, is a stern and serious kind of condemnation. Coming from the Lord Yeshua, the one who had the power to curse or bless, we can see how frustrated He was with the hypocrisy of man, who cares for what is happening on the outside and forgets that God sees the inside.

Woe, of course, simply means "May evil befall someone;" "May the worst kind of calamity befall someone." This was the curse with which Yeshua cursed the Pharisees. My prayer for you, dear reader, is that this curse will not be your portion.

Let us learn from the passage and look after the things of the heart, the things of the spirit, like love, faith, peace, mercy, compassion, justice and fair play. These will in turn lead you to do some outward and visible things that people around you would cherish.

Verses 43-44

Here, we see that the Pharisees, by the nature of their position in society as elders and leaders, were always at the forefront of every gathering. They loved and relished this position, but did not make themselves available to the people. Their position made them distance themselves from the people they ought to serve. They enjoyed the respect and accolade but not the service to the people.

The Lord compared them to a concealed tomb. What does He mean by a concealed tomb? Well, there are a lot of things a Jewish person must not go near or touch. They included people with leprosy and people with other dreadful contagious diseases. They must not touch dead bodies, coffins or even tombs where dead people are buried. So, to avoid people touching burial places and getting contaminated or unclean; such tombs were painted with white paint, making it impossible for people not to see them.

Those that were not painted in white as described above were like concealed tombs that people walked into or touched unawares. That is what the Lord compared the Pharisees to.

What a horrible comparison! He was saying that they were so deadly unclean and well-concealed that anyone who bumps into them gets contaminated so easily with their uncleanness (their teachings and ways) without knowing it.

Verses 45-46 actually make me laugh. The Lord addressed a Pharisee, a lawyer, who had said to Him, "Teacher, when you say this: you insult us too." Almost like he expected the Lord to respond apologetically: "Oh, no, no, no, I mean the Pharisees. You guys are different; not like the Pharisees." He must have been hugely disappointed because the Lord did not mince words to tell him what he thinks of the lawyers too. They thought they were something special - custodians and interpreters of the Law. They were the highly intellectual and theological minds of the time. They knew the law inside out.

Knowledge of the word of God made them proud. With the theological wrangling among them, they created more subsidiary laws to interpret the main ones. By the time they finished with it, the old law became unrecognisable. They confused ordinary people who simply wanted to know what the Law said. Their intellectual exercises did not help the people but became a hindrance to them; instead of making things easy for the people, they heaped more burden upon them and made worship more difficult.

The hypocrisy, as the Lord spotted it, was that they were not even doing what they were prescribing for the people, yet they thought of themselves as special and better than the Pharisees.

Verses 47-51

The lawyers did not kill the prophets, rather they built memorial tombs and celebrated special feast days for the dead prophets. That is not such a bad thing to do. However, what the Lord was saying was that the forefathers of the scribes and the lawyers were the same people who murdered the prophets who their children are celebrating.

The Lord was not against them building memorials and celebrating, except that the sons were no different from their fathers who killed the prophets. They were still full of all sorts of vices. If they were a bit different, then there would not be any problem, but they were not. "Sinners," the Lord seemed to be say, "are not just those who commit the sin, but include those who support and condone their sins."

Verses 49–51

> [49]Therefore the wisdom of God also said, 'I will send them prophets and apostles, and some of them they will kill and persecute,' [50]that the blood of all the prophets which was shed from the foundation of the world may be required of this generation, [51]from the blood of Abel to the blood of Zechariah who perished between the altar and the temple. Yes, I say to you, it shall be required of this generation.
>
> **(Luke 11:49-51)**

I am sure if you were present at that time you would be saying to the lawyer:

"Good for you. smart-aleck.
That serves you right.
You brought it upon yourself.
The Lord was addressing the Pharisees.
Giving them the woes due to them.
But now you redirected his attention to you the lawyers.
Good for you!
Now, you'll get your own fair share of woes".

And truly, the Lord distributed the six woes equally; three each between the Pharisees and the lawyers.

Verse 52

The last of the six woes was for the lawyers, who the Lord viewed as road-blocks; they were not going into the kingdom of God and would not let anyone else get through. Yet, as interpreters of the word of God, they were supposed to hold the key to the door to the kingdom of heaven.

All that mattered to them was:

"We are the teachers of the law
We have the key to knowledge
God is knowledge; we have the key to Him.
We stand at the door between you and God
We will show you the outside
and not the inside of heaven.
That's what we know
We are the reflection of God for you
If we can't go in, how can you?"

Verses 53-54

There are many people out there in the world who have the same attitude as the Scribes and the Pharisees. They do not like to be told the facts. They hate the truth because it hurts. In these two verses we learn that they did not like what they heard from the Lord.

They had never confronted the true nature of their spiritual life. That they had to be told about the wickedness of their ways; that they received a curse instead of a blessing, did not go down well with them. They could not handle it. Straight away, they started to plot evil against the Lord, even if it meant taking His life. In other words, "we must get rid of Him no matter what it takes."

There are many people like that in our world today. They would rather kill an opponent than to listen to constructive criticism or honest rebuke.

We all know that criticism can sometimes be hurtful, especially when it is done out of malice or bitterness. But, it is good for someone to listen to what is being said and make amends, than go deeper into iniquity either to cover up or get even.

The scribes and Pharisees were determined to get Him, and get Him they did. In doing so, they broke so many of the laws they were trying to uphold.

"Thou shall not call on the name of the Lord your God in vain." They did.

They swore in the name of God that this man had done something worthy of death. While all he did was challenge some of their erroneous beliefs and practices.

"Thou shall not kill". They did.

They knew about this commandment but were quite happy to kill him, to preserve their positions.

"Thou shall not bear false witness against thy neighbour." They did.

They even employed some professional malefactors to accuse the Lord of crimes He never committed.

My brother and sister, would you rather resort to violence when confronted with the truth? Or would you try your best to settle things amicably before it degenerates into evil and anarchy? The Bible says we should follow peace with all men and holiness; (in other words, being prepared to obey God's instructions) without which no man shall see God (Hebrews 12:14).

The question we need to ask ourselves, as we read this story of the scribes and the Pharisees is: To what extent can we go either to obey or disobey God's laws and instructions, if our jobs, positions, authority and powers are challenged? We need to meditate on this and pray that when the chips are down, we would remain on the Lord's side.

Luke Chapter 12

8

POOR, RICH HYPOCRITE

―⁕―

Luke 12:1-21

In the world in which we live, we come across lots of people who are rich in many aspects of their lives, but are poor spiritually. Some may even claim to be followers of Yahweh but in actual terms are bankrupt in the knowledge of His righteous ways of doing things. Sometimes, these are those who have a form of godliness but deny the power of God.

These are the kinds of people the Lord Yeshua encountered; like the Scribes and Pharisees. At times, He would get angry, call them names (wolves, vipers, etc) and just tell it to them as it was. Of course, it did not go down well with his hearers. When the recipients storm off in anger to go and plot how they would catch him, that left a kind of dense tension in the air, as we can see in this segment of our study entitled "Poor, Rich Hypocrite."

> [1]In the meantime, when an innumerable multitude of people had gathered together, so that they trampled one another, He began to say to His disciples first of all, "Beware of the

leaven of the Pharisees, which is hypocrisy. ²For there is nothing covered that will not be revealed, nor hidden that will not be known. ³Therefore whatever you have spoken in the dark will be heard in the light, and what you have spoken in the ear in inner rooms will be proclaimed on the housetops.

⁴"And I say to you, My friends, do not be afraid of those who kill the body, and after that have no more that they can do. ⁵But I will show you whom you should fear: Fear Him who, after He has killed, has power to cast into hell; yes, I say to you, fear Him! ⁶"Are not five sparrows sold for two copper coins? And not one of them is forgotten before God. ⁷But the very hairs of your head are all numbered. Do not fear therefore; you are of more value than many sparrows.

⁸"Also I say to you, whoever confesses Me before men, him the Son of Man also will confess before the angels of God. ⁹But he who denies Me before men will be denied before the angels of God. ¹⁰"And anyone who speaks a word against the Son of Man, it will be forgiven him; but to him who blasphemes against the Holy Spirit, it will not be forgiven. ¹¹"Now when they bring you to the synagogues and magistrates and authorities, do not worry about how or what you should answer, or what you should say. ¹²For the

Holy Spirit will teach you in that very hour what you ought to say."

¹³Then one from the crowd said to Him, "Teacher, tell my brother to divide the inheritance with me." ¹⁴But He said to him, "Man, who made Me a judge or an arbitrator over you?" ¹⁵And He said to them, "Take heed and beware of covetousness, for one's life does not consist in the abundance of the things he possesses." ¹⁶Then He spoke a parable to them, saying: "The ground of a certain rich man yielded plentifully. ¹⁷And he thought within himself, saying, 'What shall I do, since I have no room to store my crops?' ¹⁸So he said, 'I will do this: I will pull down my barns and build greater, and there I will store all my crops and my goods. ¹⁹And I will say to my soul, "Soul, you have many goods laid up for many years; take your ease; eat, drink, and be merry."' ²⁰But God said to him, 'Fool! This night your soul will be required of you; then whose will those things be which you have provided? ²¹"So is he who lays up treasure for himself, and is not rich toward God."

(Luke 12:1-21)

In verse 1, other versions (including the *King James Version*), say "Meanwhile." But I like how the *New American Standard Version* started chapter

12, considering all the commotion that had gone on before at the dinner party (chapter 11).

> [1]Under these circumstances, after so many thousands of people had gathered together that they were stepping on one another, He began saying to His disciples first of all, "Beware of the leaven of the Pharisees, which is hypocrisy.

"Under these circumstances" of the commotion and subsequent rebuke, there were thousands of people milling around who were at most stepping on each other. Here Luke, as a great storyteller, creates the picture and image on our minds of what the atmosphere was like.

It was at that critical moment that the Lord turned aside and gave His disciples one of the sternest warnings ever. He warned them of the yeast, the leaven of the Pharisees, which He said was hypocrisy.

Leaven, of course, is simply yeast, the ingredient for making dough. This ingredient makes dough rise and causes it to be bigger than it actually is. The Lord was saying to His disciples to beware of the teachings and religious lifestyle of the Pharisees. "It is hypocritical," He said. It makes them look good, and conceals what they really are. This is dangerous and leads a lot of people astray from worshipping God in spirit and in truth. That warning is true today as it was 2000 years ago when the Lord was talking to His disciples; because many Pharisees have gone into the ministry fields today.

One of the things to learn about leaven, of course, is that the effect of yeast on dough takes time. In the same way, the effect of hypocritical teaching by deceitful preachers does not show itself immediately; it takes time to manifest. Before you know it, a church is split, families are broken, relationships are smashed and backsliders are created. The Lord warns us to beware.

Verse 2
Hypocrisy is always practised undercover and pretence; never boldly in the open. The Lord is encouraging His disciples to be discerning. He reassured them that though hypocrisy works undercover, it would always be revealed for what it really is. It cannot go on hidden forever.

Verse 3 gives us a picture of some people talking in the dark, where no one could read their lips, yet all is revealed when light comes. It also gives a picture of people abandoning the living room where everyone was for the inner room, away from other people's earshot.

Nevertheless, after all that precaution, whatever they were hiding would always be made known to the public. That's what the Lord Yeshua said to His disciples and is saying to us, by way of encouragement.

Again, we meet people in life who are extremely secretive. They hold everything about themselves and their feelings close to their chest, making it hard for others to trust, confide in or relate to them. You think they are one thing but discover they are the other. That kind of lifestyle is not open, especially to friends and well-wishers. It is hypocritical and creates lack of trust.

This kind of lifestyle is not good for you or the people around you. Whatever is hidden will always come out in the open. Have an open and honest relationship with people and they would treat you the same.

Verses 4-5

These tell us of some of the stock-in-trade of the scribes and Pharisees. They trade in fear and intimidate people; they exclude people from the mainstream of society; they excommunicate worshippers from the synagogue, which was the focal point of a Jewish person's life. They can also go to the extreme of beating up or stoning people to death. From their teachings, they let their victims know that if they were not careful they would be joining other bad people in Hades – the place for the dead.

The Lord Yeshua, the Messiah, warned His disciples not to be afraid of the inflated and exaggerated teachings of the Pharisees. "They will persecute you alright; they will execute you alright; but do not be afraid of them. They can only torture your body but cannot touch your soul. So, fear no one but God; only God is capable of destroying both soul and body in hell".

Even today, some Christians do not believe in the existence of hell. It is so clear in this passage that the Lord meant hell, not Hades. We either believe Him or call Him a liar. Though hell is in the Bible and is a deterrent to those who would deliberately want to disobey God, it is not the place for those who have given their lives to the Lord and have made Him their friend. The Pharisees cannot send you there; the Lord does not want you to go there. The devil can try all he likes; he won't succeed, unless you let him.

Verses 6-7 reassures the disciples even more. However, these two verses go deeper to the heart of the disciples to address the possibility of them losing their lives for what they believe. "When you are being persecuted, you will not be alone; even unto death, you will not be forgotten by God," Yeshua reassured them.

In these two verses, the Lord painted a beautiful picture of the swoop of sparrows, which are a common occurrence on a bright sunny day in Israel. The sparrows sweep down in a park in their thousands and fly off in split seconds, making it impossible for anyone to notice any in particular, let alone count how many they were. Individually, they are so tiny in size and are seemingly of little value. When caught, their market value was only five for a farthing or two cents.

The Lord used the sparrows to teach His disciples that God never forgets His own; that they will not be forgotten if they hung unto God to the very end.

God does not forget any of the sparrows no matter how many touch-downs they make in a day. If God does not neglect tiny sparrows, how much more His beloved disciples? *"Do not fear for you are more value than any of the sparrows"* (verse 7).

That's an encouragement to you and I today.

> *"God knows you.*
> *God values and appreciates you.*
> *God acknowledges you,*
> *even when you don't feel it or hear Him say it.*
> *He will not deny you no matter what,*
> *whether in life or in death."*

However, verses 8-9 states categorically that there would be occasions when one would be expected, forced even, to declare their stand for the Lord. Some would fall away from the faith or simply deny that they knew Him. On such occasion, the Lord declared, He would not confess or present such persons before the angels in heaven. "You accept and confess me; I will accept and confess you. You deny me; I will do likewise to you."

My prayer for you my brother and my sister, dear reader, is that you will stick to God and hang on till the end, so that you would be announced and presented before the angels in heaven as a priceless bride of the Lord; that you will not have occasion to deny or be ashamed of Him; that you will listen to the teachings of the Holy Spirit, who will teach you everything you need to know about the Lord Yeshua, the Messiah.

In verse 10, the Lord says:

"Beware, they will pressure you; they will persecute you, but don't fall for their traps. They would want you to swear that you never met or heard about Me; that you should deny Me with oaths and curses. Don't do it, don't fall for it. If you do you would be lying. If you deny Me, you'll be forgiven, but if you deny what the Holy Spirit had taught you, which you know to be true, and replace it with blasphemies, oaths and curses, you will not be forgiven."

Verses 11-12

The Lord did not mince words in telling His disciples what would befall them and what they should expect. He gave them an example: "You will be dragged before the synagogues and the authorities" Why? "To deny me, of course. Do not become anxious about how or what you should speak in your defence, or what you should say; for the Holy Spirit will teach you in that very hour what you ought to say."

Yeshua was simply saying to His disciples that they should be steadfast and immoveable; have faith in God to come to their rescue; trust the teacher, the Holy Spirit to teach them the way of escape. The same He is saying to us today.

Verse 13

What happened in this verse is what I call the "let's-talk-about-something-else syndrome." This is when someone wants to change the subject of discussion because it is getting too deep for comfort. If they were bold enough, they will voice out and say, "Can we talk about something else please? Can we change the subject? It's really getting on my nerves!"

In verse 13, someone in the crowd would rather be talking about properties, stocks and shares, the whole prosperity issue, than talk about possible persecution or death. In other words, "talk to us about what we need now; don't preach to us about heaven, hell or the afterlife."

Our Lord Yeshua was a balanced teacher. He taught many times about inheritance but He balanced it out with hard teachings too. It is easy to be one-sided in the things of God in order to please an audience. But He had a mission to save as many as wanted the truth, no matter how hard. The Lord may have been many things to many people, but one hat He refused to wear was that of an arbiter, or an executor of wills for the people.

Verse 15

Here, the Lord pointed His finger at the heart of our entire human problem, the reason why people live such hypocritical lives. He explained that it was all about greed and self-indulgence; accumulation and amassing of wealth and properties here on earth. The Lord spoke to this young man, to the multitude and to His disciples. "Beware of every form of greed."

The Lord was in the world to preach and teach about eternal life, but this man wanted to talk about properties and possessions. Greed was driving a wedge between him and his brother. Surely, two brothers could amicably divide their inheritance among themselves, but the society was so sold-out on greed and self-aggrandisement that it would not be strange if a brother decided to take unto himself that which belonged to him and his kin.

In that same story, the Lord pointed out another truism: that a man's life does not consist of the abundance of what he possesses. How true this is today!

We hear stories of millionaires who commit suicide because they really did not enjoy life. They had enough of everything, but not life. Such people lived a life of pain, cover-up and hypocrisy. In the end, they became people to be pitied. People then call them "Poor, rich hypocrites."

Before their demise, if you talked to them about real life in Christ, they would probably ask you to change the subject. They would rather you were talking about wealth-creation and acquisitions. They want you to learn a thing or two from them on how to "make the kill," how to "buy and wipe them out."

In the end, it was all a matter of priority. What is it that matter to us most? The pursuit of eternal life or the pursuit of earthly wealth?

Wealth is not a bad thing in itself. However, the pursuit of it at the expense of one's soul and eternal life is definitely an error of judgement. The person that chooses to live this way automatically becomes a "poor, rich fool."

Verses 16-20

In these verses, the Lord concludes His teaching on poor, rich hypocrites, by telling them a parable, a story that drove home the lesson. In the story, a certain rich man was so overwhelmed with what he had accumulated that he could not hold it in. He had to make a total of twelve "Me, myself and I" proclamations!

It was all about him. God was not involved or mentioned anywhere. He forgot that without life we cannot enjoy the work of our hands, no matter how many barns we accumulate. He also forgot that God is the only giver of life.

Verses 21-22

Without God in our lives, we are incomplete equations whose problems cannot be solved; we would run around like headless chickens, and be like sheep without a shepherd; we will live as blind hypocritical fools and pretend that everything is perfectly alright. In the end, when we go so far, do not repent and turn around; we allow ourselves to fall off the cliff like rich, hypocritical fools. "So is the man who lays up treasure for himself and is not rich towards God" (verse 2); he is a poor, rich hypocrite.

9

STOP WORRYING, KEEP WATCHING

Luke 12:22-43

²²Then He said to His disciples, "Therefore I say to you, do not worry about your life, what you will eat; nor about the body, what you will put on. ²³Life is more than food, and the body is more than clothing. ²⁴Consider the ravens, for they neither sow nor reap, which have neither storehouse nor barn; and God feeds them. Of how much more value are you than the birds? ²⁵And which of you by worrying can add one cubit to his stature? ²⁶If you then are not able to do the least, why are you anxious for the rest? ²⁷Consider the lilies, how they grow: they neither toil nor spin; and yet I say to you, even Solomon in all his glory was not arrayed like one of these. ²⁸If then God so clothes the grass, which today is in the field and tomorrow is thrown into the oven, how much more will He clothe you, O you of little faith? ²⁹"And do not seek what

you should eat or what you should drink, nor have an anxious mind. ³⁰For all these things the nations of the world seek after, and your Father knows that you need these things. ³¹But seek the kingdom of God, and all these things shall be added to you. ³²"Do not fear, little flock, for it is your Father's good pleasure to give you the kingdom. ³³Sell what you have and give alms; provide yourselves money bags which do not grow old, a treasure in the heavens that does not fail, where no thief approaches nor moth will be also The Faithful Servant and the Evil Servant

³⁵"Let your waist be girded and your lamps burning; ³⁶and you yourselves be like men who wait for their master, when he will return from the wedding, that when he comes and knocks they may open to him immediately. ³⁷Blessedare those servants whom the master, when he comes, will find watching. Assuredly, I say to you that he will gird himself and have them sit down to eat, and will come and serve them. ³⁸And if he should come in the second watch, or come in the third watch, and find them so, blessed are those servants. ³⁹But know this, that if the master of the house had known what hour the thief would come, he would have watched and not allowed his house to be broken into. ⁴⁰Therefore you also be ready, for the Son of Man is coming at an hour you do not expect." ⁴¹Then Peter said to

Him, "Lord, do You speak this parable only to us, or to all people?" ⁴²And the Lord said, "Who then is that faithful and wise steward, whom his master will make ruler over his household, to give them their portion of food in due season? ⁴³Blessed is that servant whom his master will find so doing when he comes. ⁴⁴Truly, I say to you that he will make him ruler over all that he has. ⁴⁵But if that servant says in his heart, 'My master is delaying his coming,' and begins to beat the male and female servants, and to eat and drink and be drunk, ⁴⁶the master of that servant will come on a day when he is not looking for him, and at an hour when he is not aware, and will cut him in two and appoint him his portion with the unbelievers. ⁴⁷And that servant who knew his master's will, and did not prepare himself or do according to his will, shall be beaten with many stripes. ⁴⁸But he who did not know, yet committed things deserving of stripes, shall be beaten with few. For everyone to whom much is given, from him much will be required; and to whom much has been committed, of him they will ask the more.

(Luke 12:22-43)

In this section of Scripture, the Lord is still continuing the discourse He started at the incident in chapter 11, from verse 37; where He was invited to dinner by one of the Pharisees. At that dinner, His host practically called Him "unclean" because He did not wash Himself and do all the ceremonial things the people did before they ate.

The Lord spotted their hypocrisy and rebuked the Pharisees, including His host. The passage ends by revealing to us that from then on, they began to plot on how to catch Him on His words, to arrest Him for what He said and to kill Him.

He took His disciples aside and warned them of the hypocritical false teachings and lifestyle of the scribes and the Pharisee. He warned them not to be afraid of them. He unveiled their limitations, that they can only punish or persecute the body, but cannot destroy the soul. The disciples were to be fearless and steadfast to the end. Even if they lose their lives, they will get it back in heaven. They were only to fear God, who is able to destroy both body and soul.

They were not to deny Him here on earth because if they did, He would deny them also in heaven, in the presence of His Heavenly Father and the angels. He warned them that the worst the Pharisees could do was kick them out from normal society and excommunicate them from assembling in the synagogue.

They may even force them to be destitute, with no property, food or clothes to wear. In spite of all these, Yeshua said to them, "Fear not."

Verse 22

> Then He said to His disciples, "Therefore I say to you, do not worry about your life, what

you will eat; nor about the body, what you will put on.

(Luke 12:22)

We are being taught here that it is fear that causes anxiety. People worry about what they would eat in order to look good; what they would wear in order to look good. Even when people display what they have (in terms of properties, cars, yachts, jewelleries and other things), it is for the purpose of looking good before other people. But the Lord says: "Don't worry, keep watch and be ready."

Verse 22 also reveals to us that though human beings are always anxious of what they would eat and what they would put on, there is also a third dimension of anxiety that they pay less attention to. This is the dimension of the soul. We spend most of our lives looking after the first and second dimensions of existence (the physical accumulation of goods and properties), to the detriment of the third dimension (the nourishment of our souls) where true life is centred. Hence, the Lord's statement in verse 23.

In verse 24, the Lord Yeshua, in His imitable way of teaching, brought into their imagination the picture of a raven to show how precious the disciples were in the sight of God. I don't know why He chose the ravens; they are not the most colourful or decorated of birds. Perhaps that's why He chose them. They don't do too much running helter-skelter in search of food and clothing like we do. They don't build barns to accumulate wealth like we do, but they are never in want; they are well-fed and lack nothing.

Again, when we look with our physical eyes only, we miss out on a lot of things. The raven is a greyish or black-feathered bird, but the Creator of all things chose this blandly coloured bird to show us that there's more to the raven than meets the eye. It is definitely well looked after.

Verses 25-26
I find these verses fascinating. Human beings who run around, sow and reap, store their surplus and accumulate abundance, all for the sake of food, clothing and the pride of life, die eventually. They are not able, even with the wealth they have amassed, to extend their lives by even a dot of a second beyond their allotted time on earth.

Birds on the other hand (using the raven as an example) do not live with anxiety as to where the next food is going to come from or where they will get the right clothes for the next occasion. Like man, in the end, the bird dies. It lived and died according to the allotted time given to it by God. Just like man, it did not have the power to extend its life for a second bit. Period.

However, what intrigues me the most is what the Lord said at the tail end of verse 26. He said to the people, "If you are not able to do this, which is the least of what God can do, why bother breaking your tiny little heads worrying about other stuff?" (my paraphrase, of course).

To think that what is the most difficult for human beings to do, that is, the extension of their life span on earth), is the least for God, is fascinating to comprehend.

I am not sure if the Lord was being sarcastic here, in showing us the depth of our limitations. Whatever the case, it amused me. The Lord Yeshua, in essence, said to them that the thing that is most difficult for human beings to do is the least difficult for God to do. So, what is the point in living with anxiety when you have no control over the extension or the stoppage of life? Why not, instead, prepare the third dimension, the soul, so that whatever happens and whenever it happens, your soul will be safe and secure in the hands of God?

Why worry about what the scribes and Pharisees might do to you? Why worry about anyone for that matter if your life is not in their hands? If they persecute or even kill you, they were able to do so because God allowed it. Surely, it will not be your end, because God is the only one who has the power to extend your life, even after physical death.

Verses 27-28

The first comparison the Lord made with human beings was with animals (verses 25-26). This second comparison is with plants, lilies in particular. The Lord was saying that if we looked at the lilies by the way side, we would see an array of beautifully decorated flowers. They don't spin or weave in order to clothe themselves with the finest linen. God does it for them. If God can do it for flowers, He will do far more for you, child of God. Wouldn't He?

"As a matter of fact," the Lord said, "they are more dressed up than even Solomon, the richest and wisest man that ever lived." Why? Because God feeds and dresses them up.

I am sure that scientists are able to reveal more on what the Lord said regarding the decorations of lilies. They don't worry about anything; God feeds and decorates them. Don't worry about it, child of God; the Lord will feed and clothe you. If He can look after birds and lilies; How much more will He look after you, child of God?

Verses 29-30

> [29]"And do not seek what you should eat or what you should drink, nor have an anxious mind. [30]For all these things the nations of the world seek after, and your Father knows that you need these things.

(Luke 12:29,30)

Eating and drinking is not such a bad thing. However, they can only satisfy the needs of the flesh, and not the whole being. Those who do not know God as their Father and Provider run after these things. They are ruled by "other kingdoms" and nations where there are no promises and guarantees. But you have a heavenly Father, Yahweh Jireh, who knows "that you have need for these things."

Verses 31-32

Since the discourse, teachings and warnings that started in chapter 11, these two verses are for me, the central and focal point of what Yeshua was communicating. "Seek the Kingdom, get into it, make sure you're in, once you are in, you are a citizen; not only that; you are the son or daughter of the King who rules the Kingdom. You are royalty and will be provided for, as long as you believe and act like one."

In all your getting, dear reader, get the most important thing – the Kingdom of Heaven. Also, be rest assured that God does not want to prevent you from entering, for verse 32 says: "Fear not, little flock, for it is your father's good pleasure to give you the kingdom." He is not doing it grudgingly, No! It is His "good pleasure," to accept you into the kingdom of heaven, only by you accepting Yeshua the Messiah as your entrance ticket. Think about the most important thing in the whole wide world; the kingdom of heaven, that's what God, your heavenly Father is willing to give you access into.

Seek and you will find Him
Knock and the doors swing open
Sit comfortably and you will be served
You will be clothed, you will be sheltered.

Verses 33-36

These verses teach us to open and start saving in a new bank account in heaven. The banks here on earth cannot guarantee the growth or security of our savings. With just one economic downturn or crisis, earthly investments can get wiped out completely. Thieves could go into banks and rob us of our savings; moths could "go in" and destroy our shares and bonds; the chip or hard drive where our details are stored can be stolen.

The bank of heaven, on the other hand, is not accessible to thieves, moths or any other agent of destruction. We are admonished, therefore, to pile up our savings in this heavenly bank, thus tuning our minds towards heaven; "for where your treasure is, there will your heart be also" (verse 34).

It is important to note that this heavenly bank, so to speak, does not trade in stocks, shares and mortgages. It does not trade with Dollars, Pound Sterling, Naira or any earthly currency. It only accepts savings of one priceless commodity – LOVE. "Love the Lord God with all your heart, with your entire mind and with all your strength" (Deuteronomy 6:5).

Verse 33 of our text in Luke says: "Sell your possessions and give in love (or rather 'give love') to others; then you would have opened an account in heaven where the purses or containers do not rot, decay or get overwhelmed." Giving of love is the source of unfailing treasure in heaven.

To have treasure in heaven means our hearts and our minds will be towards heaven all the time. We would be full of great anticipation. The thought of heaven will no longer be that of dread and fearful apprehension, but of great expectation of the day to "cash in" on our savings.

Verses 35-37 is mostly talking about our readiness to go on the spur of the moment. If we had our treasures stored up in heaven, our readiness will be intensified, seeing we have little or no investment here on the earth. We should be like the bride of the Lord, who cannot wait to be swept off her feet.

Verses 37-38 says there's no need for us to spend too much time speculating when this eminent arrival of the master was going to come. What is certain is that whenever it happens, all the children of God who have been on alert, will not miss out on His appearing. They will be looked after. They will be well pampered and "spoiled" with the glory of heaven. It could happen any moment from now – morning, noon or night. When exactly, we don't know; but whoever is ready when He comes will be greatly blessed and highly favoured.

Verses 39-40
We are taught here that the Lord knows what He is doing by keeping the knowledge of the time of His arrival from us. If we knew in advance the date and time of His arrival, we would take that time for granted and only concentrate to serve the Lord and wait on Him at the very last minute; but no one knows the day or the time.

> ^{39}But know this, that if the master of the house had known what hour the thief would come, he would have watched and not allowed his house to be broken into. ^{40}Therefore you also

be ready, for the Son of Man is coming at an hour you do not expect."

(Luke 12:39,40)

Verses 41-42

The things the Lord was talking about here resembled what a master would be saying to his servants in private when he is about to embark on a long journey. No wonder Peter chipped in to seek clarification. "Lord, are you addressing this parable about going away, coming back suddenly and readiness to us your disciples or are you speaking to the general public as well?"

The Lord made it clear to Peter and the rest of the disciples that He was addressing the chief stewards who would be left in charge looking after and feeding the rest of the people. He was also addressing everyone else who will follow His teachings, which they would receive through the apostles. All He wanted was a truly faithful group of disciples who will serve Him when He was present as well as in His absence.

Verses 43-45

These verses reiterate the fact that as Christians, we have a Master. He is the Lord over everything and everyone. Leaders in His Church, whether they be apostles, bishops, pastors or any other designation, are only supervisors appointed by the Lord. They are not the Lord Himself. They should, therefore, be careful not to treat the people in their care as if they belonged to them personally. Self-serving leadership and being power-drunk are unacceptable to the Lord.

Verses 46-48

Yeshua, by virtue of being the Master, is in charge of His own travels. We do not control Him. So, He was not going to tell His servants the exact time of His return. The Lord warned that supervisors can misuse their power and maltreat those under their care. The Lord put it in no uncertain terms that any supervisor caught behaving out of sorts will be punished severely: "flogged with floggings, not just a few."

Remember that Peter wanted to know whether these teachings and injunctions were for the general public or exclusively for them—apostles and disciples. Well, here in verse 48, the Lord explained to Peter and to the rest of the people that whether you are an apostle or a disciple, you will be judged according to your position; in accordance with the level of your appointment and responsibility.

We can imply from this teaching that "uneasy lies the head that wears the crown." Leadership is not a bed of roses. The higher you go, the higher your responsibilities and reward; much more will be required of you by way of accountability.

Also the higher your position, the greater the magnitude of your punishment compared to those who have no specific portfolio. That is what the Lord communicated to Peter, the disciples and the rest of us today. So, let us stop worrying, keep on watching and be ready for His return.

10

PRINCE OF PEACE, LORD OF DIVISION

Luke 12:49-59

Long before the Lord Yeshua was born into the world as a man, the prophet Isaiah declared by revelation that He will be called, amongst other names, the Prince of Peace (Isaiah 9:6).

This same Isaiah prophesied that "the chastisement of our peace was upon Him" (Isaiah 53:5). In other words, the punishment and suffering that we were to receive was laid upon Him, in exchange for peace.

When He was born, the Bible records that the angels proclaimed that He will bring praise to God and secure peace for all men. This implied that the Messiah will deal with the root of commotion, confusion, rebellion, resentment and wars, which is the lack of peace.

Fundamentally, in all eras of human existence, the lack of peace had posed the most questions. And unanswered questions unsettle the mind more than anything else, thus breeding a lack of peace in our lives. "Who am I? Where am I going to? Where am I coming from? What is truth? Is there life after death? Is there a heaven and a hell?" Questions like these abound, but their answers can be found in Yeshua, in a single statement that He made about Himself:

> "I am the way, the truth and the life. No one comes to the Father except through me."

(John 14:6)

All the questions of mankind were answered in this single declaration; and no other human being, alive or dead, has ever made a claim that matches this one.

The Lord Yeshua brought us answers to all our nagging questions, thereby giving us the peace that was missing in our lives. By this feat, He has truly become our Prince of Peace. By answering questions that no one had answers to, He brought us peace from heaven above.

God and the people were once at enmity with each other. But the Lord Yeshua became the bridge-builder, the peace-maker, and the mediator between God and man. He brought them together again in friendship and love.

Yeshua said, "I am *the Way*," because as the Mediator, He was the only way of negotiation back to the Father. Once you get to know the Father through Him, you will have the peace in your soul and spirit "that passes all understanding." (Philippians 4:7).

Yeshua also said, "I am *the Truth*." Since the fall, man has been groping in the dark in search of truth.

The truth is God's way of thinking and acting, and the Lord Yeshua is the exact representation of God's word and ways. The minute we realise this, that same minute we will have peace.

God was not lying when He said He would send a Redeemer, for He is not a man that He should lie. This was clearly revealed at the coming of our Lord Yeshua, sent of God to save the whole world; and that is the truth.

Yeshua said, "I am *the Life*." One of the worries of our existence, one that disturbs our peace is the issue of life after death. "What happens after we die?" Whatever people had postulated on this subject before the arrival of the Lord Yeshua, were mere conjectures. Nobody knew anything for sure. But the Lord came and reassured the people that there is life after death, and that He was the assurance of it. This He was sure of; He was not guessing at all.

Without Him there is no life for us in heaven. Without Him there will be no peace in the world and in the world to come. Anyone who receives Him will not perish but have eternal life. The Lord Yeshua fulfilled this promise and became the answer to all our questions at the same time.

In these instances, the Lord Yeshua filled in the blank spaces that disturbed our peace. He became our peace when He broke down every wall of partition that was blocking our relationship with God. He became the Prince of Peace; the chastisement that brought us peace was placed upon Him; and with His stripes we are healed.

Prince of Peace, Lord of Division

The disciples had already learned and settled it in their hearts that the Lord Yeshua was the Prince of Peace, when, all of a sudden, He turned the teaching notch one level higher, and declared to His disciples that He was also the Lord of divisions.

Division, as we all know, causes chaos and a lack of peace. How could the Lord be the Prince of peace and the Lord of division at the same time? What does the Lord mean by these sayings?

> [49]"I came to send fire on the earth, and how I wish it were already kindled! [50]But I have a baptism to be baptized with, and how distressed I am till it is accomplished! [51]Do you suppose that I came to give peace on earth? I tell you, not at all, but rather division. [52]For from now on five in one house will be divided: three against two, and two against three. [53]Father will be divided against son and son against father, mother against daughter and daughter against mother, mother-in-law against her daughter-in-law and daughter-in-law against her mother-in-law."

> [54]Then He also said to the multitudes, "Whenever you see a cloud rising out of the west, immediately you say, 'A shower is coming'; and so it is. [55]And when you see the south wind blow, you say, 'There will be hot weather'; and there is. [56]Hypocrites! You can discern the face of the sky and of the earth, but how is it you do not discern this time?

⁵⁷"Yes, and why, even of yourselves, do you not judge what is right? ⁵⁸When you go with your adversary to the magistrate, make every effort along the way to settle with him, lest he drag you to the judge, the judge deliver you to the officer, and the officer throw you into prison. ⁵⁹I tell you, you shall not depart from there till you have paid the very last mite."

(Luke 12:49-59)

Verse 49

In this verse, our Prince of Peace makes a declaration to the people that He had come to set fire upon the earth; and He wished it had already started. We knew Him as the Prince of Peace but now He is taking on a new role as the Lord of Division, and He wants to accomplish this by setting fire upon the earth.

First of all, it must be understood that there are various mentions of fire in the Bible, majority of which are symbolic. This verse is one of such symbolisms. What the Lord was referring to as fire was His teachings, doctrines, and His new way of seeing and doing things. The Lord was hinting that what He brought was new and different. It kindles like fire; and when it kindles, some major old furniture will be consumed along the way.

The Lord had been teaching his disciples and the general public now for nearly three years. As He taught and mingled with the people, He was gradually kindling the fire. However, at the time when He made this statement, the fire of His teachings had not been fully ignited among His disciples, let alone on the multitude.

We can understand, then, what the Lord meant by His statement. He wished the fire of His Gospel was already kindled all over the world while He was still teaching in the midst of them. We know that this fire did not blaze to the full until the day of Pentecost, when the Holy Ghost fell upon the disciples and fanned the burning embers unto the "uttermost parts of the earth."

Let there be no doubt as to what kind of fire Yeshua was referring to here. Surely, it was not physical fire. Remember that God had promised not to destroy the world again with water. Well, it may be by fire; however, He was not talking about a destructive fire in verse 49, He was talking about a *reconstructive* fire that is capable of rattling the status quo.

The Lord was teaching us about the powerful force that the Gospel is. He wants us to know that the fire of His Gospel will be more powerful than any ideology that the world had ever known. He wanted His disciples to get prepared before it actually started to blaze.

And so it was, after the feast of Pentecost, when the Holy Ghost fell upon the disciples, that the Gospel of the Kingdom of God spread more than any wild fire that had ever been kindled. It captured minds and spirits. It consumed obstacles on its way into nations and lands beyond Israel. It is still raging on even to this day.

Verse 50

The Lord told His disciples that before the fire starts in its full strength, He would need to undergo a form of baptism. In this case, we now know it was the baptism of suffering.

The use of the word baptism in the Bible is, again, one that is largely symbolic, allowing the reader to meditate and discover the depth of what is being taught. This must not be misunderstood with our modern usage of the word baptism. Here in verse 50, the Lord was not talking about water baptism as proclaimed by John the Baptist. Rather, He was speaking of a process, a passing through of something after which His task would be accomplished. This is similar to how the children of Israel were "baptised into Moses." They were immersed into all that Moses stood for, the crossing of the parted Red Sea being the climax.

Baptism, therefore, including the one referred to here in verse 50, is the total immersing of one's self into something; a commitment and a burying of oneself into a cause. The Lord was talking about the baptism of suffering, which He must commit His soul and body to, even to the very end. He must suffer in the hands of His enemies until He is able to say, "It is finished."

Even though the Lord desired the fire of His teachings to have started spreading all around the world, He said, "But I have a baptism to be baptised with." This is a big "But," and with it, the Lord Yeshua was teaching us about patience.

Every process in life has its own time. We cannot jump the sequence of how things work. We cannot choose the pleasant and exciting processes of life when some not-so-pleasant ones precede them. The prospect of the Gospel spreading all over the world like wild fire was surely a sweeter experience to look forward to than the baptism of suffering that the Lord had to first endure.

The spreading of the Gospel, therefore, is not laid on a bed of roses. There is the baptism of suffering attached to it. Most of the time this baptism comes first before the fruit of your labour in the Lord's vineyard. And it is hardly a pain-free affair. Instead, it is full of distress and despair. When you encounter these, dear reader, do not worry, the Lord also felt distressed and wished it was already over and done with. Never give up on your baptism of suffering because it is the only pathway to glory and fulfilment.

Verses 51-53

These verses reveal that the Lord was beginning to challenge some of the bottled-up assumptions that the Messiah will be the Prince of Peace who will usher in tranquillity in Israel by defeating all the enemies and oppressors of the Jews.

What a shock it must have been to their system to hear the Lord say to them that this was not His mission. As we considered earlier, He did not cease being the Prince of Peace; but the kind of peace that His teachings would produce would cause division in the world. The Jews were focusing on themselves but the Lord Yeshua intimated them that He was thinking about the whole world. "Do you suppose that I came 'to grant peace on earth'?" (verse 51).

There are two things for us to learn from this verse: Firstly, God is for the whole world. Whenever He makes plans, He considers the entire world, and not just your little community. Even though the Jews are God's chosen people, He still loves the rest of the world, especially those who have come to know Him through Yeshua, the Messiah.

The second thing to learn from this passage is that opposites always abide by each other to produce a desired end—war and peace, unity and division, male and female, good and bad, rich and poor etc. And in most cases, one aspect would need to be prominent before you miss the other. Before we know the value of good, bad will reign for a season. Before we appreciate freedom and independence, maltreatment in exile might be the antidote to propel us into praying for freedom and independence.

In this passage, Yeshua warned the people of what was going to happen: "When you see what commotion and division My teaching will cause around the world; when you see how principalities and powers will rise up and go to war to oppose it; then you will know the value of the peace I bring, how precious it is and why the enemy does not want you to have it."

In verse 52, the Lord went down to the nitty-gritty to explain to His disciples and the crowd following Him what He meant by such a seemingly negative statement. He explained that from that moment onwards, what He brought into the world, "the good news of great joy to all mankind," would create misunderstandings, quarrels and division in people's households.

Verse 53 brought it home even further. The Lord was saying: "Listen, I am not talking about distant relations or extended family. I am actually talking about father and son, mother and daughter, mother in-law and father in-law. I am talking, 'that close'. They will not all agree to follow the new life I have brought for them."

At the time He was speaking, majority of the people were deeply laden with the "leaven of the Pharisees," and would have found it very difficult to break free. The Pharisees, essentially, controlled people's lives.

So, what the Lord Yeshua was warning His disciples about was for them to be prepared to live lives full of integrity. For them to realise that life ahead was going to be tough; at a time when people would be compelled to declare one way or the other. Are you for Moses and Yahweh or are you for Yeshua and Yahweh? Whichever one you choose, there would be conflict. Only stand firm with the Lord Yeshua.

It is all about conviction, isn't it? You can only commit your life to what you are well persuaded of. The Lord was saying to His disciples, just like His namesake Joshua said to the children of Israel in the desert, "Choose you this day who you will serve, the divine teaching from the One who came from above or the hypocritical doctrines of the Pharisees. You choose. You must be warned; you must be determined. Division will come."

Verses 54-56

At this moment, the Lord turned His attention specifically to the multitude, especially those following as spectators. These ones were not really taking His teachings in, nor were they observing the sign of the times. They could not sense what was about to happen, how His teaching was going to unleash persecution and division among peoples and nations.

The Lord Yeshua was saying to the crowd: "How come you know how to read the weather and the signs of the season, but when it comes to reading the sign for the impending danger to your soul, you have no clue whatsoever? How come you can predict correctly that it would soon rain as soon as you see a little cloud forming in the West? You quite easily predict that it would be a hot day just because you felt the south wind from the desert blowing on your face?

How come you know all these signs and when you interpret them, you are always right? How come, you can't see the sign of the moment? How come you can't read the handwriting on the wall concerning your own lives? Can you not see the impending danger?"

How true these questions are in our lives and society today! Is it not true that there are millions of well-educated men and women milling around in the world who know everything there is to know about everything else, but have no clue about the salvation of their own souls? They research everything; prove everything by empirical materials of science, but have no idea about the condition of their soul and the spiritual dimension of life.

Verse 56 (NAB)

"You hypocrites! You know how to analyse the appearance of the earth and sky, but why do you not analyse this present time? Are you oblivious to it or are you lying to yourselves?"

Verse 57 then asks: "And why aren't you honest enough to judge what is right. Why can't you pick up courage, stand on the side of integrity and support what you know to be right? You have heard me preach and teach everywhere. Compared to the doctrine of the Pharisees, what do you think? If you told the truth of what you feel, there will definitely be persecutions and divisions but why can't you predict this as you do with all other things; to stand on the side of truth; knowing that it is inevitable and it frees?"

Verses 58-59

We have been taught earlier by the Lord Yeshua that there is only one ultimate Judge, God in heaven, who is able to cast both body and soul into hell. If anyone is cast into hell, unfortunately, there is no remedy, no eventual release, and no amount of redemptive prayers offered by the living or indulgencies that can bring the person out of hell and into heaven.

In these verses, the Lord warned and admonished the people to make the right decision and choose the righteous Judge rather than wait for his final judgement. He said to them, "Read the signs, make peace now before it is too late." Just like David wrote in one of his Messianic Psalms, the Lord warned the people:

"Be wise now therefore you Kings; be instructed, you judges of the earth. Serve the Lord with fear, and rejoice with trembling. Kiss the Son, lest He be angry, and ye perish from the way, when His wrath is kindled but a little Blessed are all they that put their trust in Him."

(Psalm 2:10-12)

The Lord's warning was not just to the disciples and the multitude that gathered to hear Him; this warning is still relevant to us today. As we consider the signs of the season, let us settle and make peace with the Prince of peace now before it is too late. It is not worth missing the flight to heaven. Worst still, there is the danger of being dragged, kicking and screaming, to a place of the Lord's anger and punishment where there will be no chance of release. You will also not be able to pay your debts, even the barest farthen.

So, do not ignore the signs of the End Time, which are so clearly visible in our present age. Do something about your life today before it is too late. Accept the Lord Yeshua, the Messiah, as your Lord and Saviour, so it may be well with you. Repent and ask Him for forgiveness and He will graciously pardon you. You will have life and peace and you will have it more abundantly. You will be a child of God, loved by God and protected by God, your Father.

The Lord seriously admonished the people to repent and seek God while He may be found. It is the same thing He is saying to you and I today.

Luke Chapter 13

11

LORD, WHY ME?

Luke 13:1-22

When calamity and tragedy strikes, we usually find ourselves asking, "Lord, why me?" If it happens to people far from us, we may ask, "Lord, why them?", but when we do, the thought will probably last a few moments in our minds after which we carry on with our daily business and forget all about the disaster completely.

Not only do we ask the question, "Lord, why me?" when affected by tragedy, we ask it over and over for the major part of our lives, especially if the calamity involves a young person, or a loved one on whom we have pinned our hopes of future progress. We carry on asking the same question as if we would have preferred it happened to someone else.

The trouble is, there has hardly been an answer to this aged question that has satisfied enquirers; people really do not hear what they would like to hear at such times, an explanation that will take the pain in their heart away.

I remember years ago, a friend of mine, Bishop David Titus, a true servant of God in my opinion.

He served God and his fellow man all around the world. He went from nation to nation; from city to city, preaching the Gospel of the Kingdom of God and mobilising ministers together to do the work of God. He did all this everywhere but when he focused on doing the same in his own country, Nigeria, he was tragically killed in a crossfire between police and armed robbers on the streets of Lagos. He was driving past, minding his own business, when tragedy struck.

In a situation like this, not only his wife and children asked, "Lord, why him?" Many who knew him, including myself, asked the same thing. This was clearly the case, judging by the thousands who attended his funeral in London.

Again, I remember another good friend of mine; a lady minister of God, Rev Elaine David. She was a preacher, teacher and musician; a truly humble servant of God, going from ministry to ministry, sometimes with her husband, Val, ministering in word and songs.

All of a sudden, Elaine was diagnosed with a blood disease that resulted in her being bedridden in hospital. It wasn't long before Pastor Elaine David was gone from us. The question was, "Lord, why her?" "We know from her fruit and her work, that she was a true servant of God but Lord, why her? Why did she have to go so early?"

There are also some servants of God I know, "over 17 years ago (whether in the body or out of the body, I cannot tell; God knows—2 Cor 12:2)" who went about doing their work in the body of Christ, as they believed God had called them to do. All of a sudden, one of their daughters was diagnosed as autistic and having a learning disability. They could not think of any reason why this should happen, seeing they were going about doing God's work.

As they watched their daughter grow up into a woman with this disability, what was the question they asked daily? Of course, "Lord, why us?" "Lord, why her?"

We can ask these questions as much as we like, but funny enough, the Lord does not give us the kind of answers that we expect or would like to hear. That's what we will see in the scripture segment we are about to study.

> [1]There were present at that season some who told Him about the Galileans whose blood Pilate had mingled with their sacrifices. [2]And Jesus answered and said to them, "Do you suppose that these Galileans were worse sinners than all other Galileans, because they suffered such things? [3]I tell you, no; but unless you repent you will all likewise perish. [4]Or those eighteen on whom the tower in Siloam fell and killed them, do you think that they were worse sinners than all other men who dwelt in Jerusalem? [5]I tell you, no; but unless you repent you will all likewise perish."
>
> [6]He also spoke this parable: "A certain man had a fig tree planted in his vineyard, and he came seeking fruit on it and found none. [7]Then he said to the keeper of his vineyard,

'Look, for three years I have come seeking fruit on this fig tree and find none. Cut it down; why does it use up the ground?' [8]But he answered and said to him, 'Sir, let it alone this year also, until I dig around it and fertilize it. [9]And if it bears fruit, well. But if not, after that you can cut it down.'" [10]Now He was teaching in one of the synagogues on the Sabbath. [11]And behold, there was a woman who had a spirit of infirmity eighteen years, and was bent over and could in no way raise herself up. [12]But when Jesus saw her, He called her to Him and said to her, "Woman, you are loosed from your infirmity." [13]And He laid His hands on her, and immediately she was made straight, and glorified God. [14]But the ruler of the synagogue answered with indignation, because Jesus had healed on the Sabbath; and he said to the crowd, "There are six days on which men ought to work; therefore come and be healed on them, and not on the Sabbath day." [15]The Lord then answered him and said, "Hypocrite! Does not each one of you on the Sabbath loose his ox or donkey from the stall, and lead it away to water it? [16]So ought not this woman, being a daughter of Abraham, whom Satan has bound—think of it—for eighteen years, be loosed from this bond on the Sabbath?" [17]And when He said these things, all His adversaries were put to shame; and all the multitude rejoiced for all the glorious things that were done by Him.

^{18}Then He said, "What is the kingdom of God like? And to what shall I compare it? ^{19}It is like a mustard seed, which a man took and put in his garden; and it grew and became a large tree, and the birds of the air nested in its branches." ^{20}And again He said, "To what shall I liken the kingdom of God? ^{21}It is like leaven, which a woman took and hid in three measures of meal till it was all leavened." ^{22}And He went through the cities and villages, teaching, and journeying toward Jerusalem.

(Luke 13:1-22)

Verse 1 says: "Now on the same occasion there were some present that intimated to Him about the Galileans, whose blood Pilate had mingled with his sacrifices."

On the same occasion, what occasion? We must bear in mind the people that were crowding the Lord day and night as He preached. These were Jews who had waited all their lives for the Messiah that would come and deliver them from their oppressors; Jews who were expecting a hero and an avenger who would repay the Romans for all the evil they had committed against them.

But picking up from Chapter 11, all they had heard so far was not encouraging. Yeshua had told them that the Pharisees were leading people astray; that those who refuse to follow them would be persecuted; "As for me, I will be betrayed and handed over to them, to be tortured and killed. Stay calm, let not your heart be troubled, believe in God, believe also in Me." This was not what they "bargained for," so to speak. They expected much more from their conquering Messiah.

Just in case He was the Messiah but did not understand why He came, there were some in the crowd, on the same occasion, that drew His attention to the real issues—the oppression and evils of the Romans. They found His discourse gruesome and took it upon themselves to point out some "pressing matters" to Him.

As long as the Lord preached and proclaimed the Kingdom of God that "is at hand," every Jew wanted to test Him out to know if He was the Expected One. They did this through the questions they asked Him, noting each time how He answered and reacted. Since what He seemed to major upon was too personal, they practically changed the subject to more general issues.

They decided to bring it home to Him. If they talked to Him about any other town or city in Israel, where the Romans had wickedly done great evils against the people, he may not feel it that much, they thought. "But if we remind Him of those evils perpetrated against His own people of Galilee, then He must surely boil up in anger and do some miraculous damage against the Romans."

"The people that Pilate killed and mingled their blood in his sacrifices were Galileans. They may have come from any of the towns of Galilee; perhaps Nazareth, who knows. Whatever the case, Galilee is close to home; it should strike a chord and kindle the flame of His anger. Let's change the subject and talk about the reason why you are here, if you are indeed the Christ."

They were more of a politically-minded bunch than a spiritually-minded lot.

Verses 2-6

The people who made the comments above thought they were clever. "We will now throw Him off course by changing the subject." But the Lord shocked them by the kind of answer that He gave them. Instead of boiling in anger against Pilate and the Romans for the evil they had done; instead of saying 'O yeah, I've heard that story; yeah, that Pilate, he will get what's coming to him soon!" Instead He took the story back to His teaching and discourse regarding spiritual salvation as against physical salvation.

He made it clear to them that they will all die, one way or the other; it was only a matter of how and when; because it has been appointed unto man to die once and after that, the judgement. (Hebrews 9:27). He asked them a question, which they were not able to answer. He gave them the answer.

Verses 1-2

"Put your mind at ease; it was not because they were the worst sinners in the land at the time that Pilate killed them and used their blood for his sacrifices."

"But that's not really the main issue. The main issue is repentance, righteousness and being at peace with God. If they were in right-standing with God before Pilate killed them, what would it matter? But if they were not, they would have suffered for nothing. That's why you need to repent and reconcile with God, otherwise you will all likewise perish. It's by God's grace that you are not all consumed."

Many people in the world today make foolish assumptions that God is like a toothless bull dog that cannot do anything, one way or the other. They bring up stories of wars, atrocities, man's inhumane acts against other men, and they say if God was a just God, He would have intervened or at least pay the perpetrators back with their own coins. They conclude, therefore, that God is no longer in control, if He ever was. Even some go to the extreme of saying that He does not exist.

If He exists, how could He watch and do nothing when all the evil is going on in the world? These deep-felt questions may be sincere, however, the Lord encourages us to have faith in God, concentrate on being in right-standing with Him, and in the end, we will understand better.

Some have decided to delay their repentance from sin because of the evil going on. They have said, "There's still time to repent, definitely not now. The Lord has delayed His coming. I have enough time before He comes (if He does come), to repent." This is a dangerous assumption, because no one knows when tragedies and calamities will happen; whether it will come from man or from natural disaster.

The Lord was saying to them; "Forget the Romans; forget those who do all manner of evil; just repent from your own sins and save your own souls before it is too late. God's delay in coming is actually for your own good, to give you the chance to repent. His delay is not a sign of weakness on His part."

> "The Lord is not slow about His promise, as some count slowness, but is patient towards you, not wishing for any to perish but for all to come to repentance. But the day of the Lord will come like a thief, in which the heavens will pass away with a roar and the elements will be destroyed with intense heat, and the earth and its works will be burned up. Since all these things are to be destroyed in this way, what sort of people ought you to be in holy conduct and godliness."
>
> **(2 Peter 3:9-11 NASB)**

In many circumstances in the world, people are ready to point fingers at other people's sins and short-comings rather than deal with their own. In this passage, the Lord redirected the problem to the individual rather than to the rulers. He is saying the same to you today, dear reader: *"Unless you repent, you will all likewise perish"* (verse 5).

Verses 6-7
In these verses, the Lord started to tell them a story to buttress what He had been talking to them about. For Him, in the final analysis, it's all about occupying till He comes and bearing fruit while we occupy. In this parable, some scholars say he was

talking about Jerusalem (Israel), while others say He was talking about individuals in the crowd.

In any case, both interpretations may be right. Israel, as the chosen people of God, were a choice possession, His bride, His special tree planted to show the rest of the world who He was. They had not pleased Him, neither had they done His will. Then again, Israel is a nation and it is the individuals that make the nation who will be judged.

Bringing it down to the individual level, even into our time today, the story fits perfectly. What is Yeshua saying to us? "You are the fig tree, my special fruit-bearing tree. I am planting you in my garden, the earth. When I come checking, I expect to find the fruit of righteousness in you."

"If I come to harvest and see no fruit, I would not be pleased. However, because I am a gracious God, I would be prepared to give you a bit more time; hopefully you would start producing the desired fruit. However, if no fruit is borne, I would have no alternative than to cut you down and destroy you completely – because you would have been a waste of space."

Verses 10-13

One day, the Lord was teaching in the synagogue. It was a Sabbath day. The people did not mind that He taught, but when He disrupted His teaching to show compassion on a sick woman who had been oppressed by a spirit for eighteen years, the synagogue leaders found His actions unacceptable.

The woman had been oppressed by a spirit of infirmity for many years. As children of God today, we are to resist the devil and his spirits in the name of the Lord Yeshua. When we do, he will flee from us. For some reason, this woman could not defeat the enemy that oppressed her, and the devil made his home in her for eighteen years.

The victim in the end becomes a regular sight; the status quo; the way things are. Her condition disappears in the minds of other worshippers. Some will even blame the victim for her prayerlessness or her unconfessed sins which, supposedly, had caused the sickness.

This may or may not be the case, as the Lord made it clear in another passage (Luke 9:2-3). But even if it was due to the victim's sins, it is equally because of the weakness of the synagogue leaders that she had remained in their face for that length of time without being healed. How can an unclean spirit feel at home among them for so long? In this light, we cannot blame the victim.

The passage teaches that God loves us so much and wants to make us whole. Yeshua demonstrated how important we are to Him, by healing the woman in the middle of His preaching. Besides, the ministry of preaching and other aspects of God's work are for people anyway.

The synagogue leaders were not happy that Yeshua healed in their presence, because it was something they couldn't do themselves. To make matters worse, He did the healing on a Sabbath day.

The law forbid people toiling all week without a rest. God did not like that because it revealed that the people did not trust Him to provide for them. For this reason, He ordered them to take a day off in the week to rest and meditate on His goodness. It was for man's good that God instituted the Sabbath day.

Jesus knew why the Sabbath was instituted; to do well to man's body, soul and spirit; to give it wholeness, peace and prosperity. And when He saw that the woman did not have any of these for eighteen years, He was filled with compassion and healed her instantly.

Moreover, the Bible tells us that God does not get tired or weary; He does not sleep nor slumber. Since this is the case, we can understand why the Lord Yeshua did not need the observance of the Sabbath rest before healing the woman. Besides, the Sabbath is for man's good and not for God. Even though, when we rest and meditate on the goodness of God towards us, (while refreshing our physical bodies), God will not watch you suffer while others are having their Sabbath rest.

The woman was made well. She stood erect and started praising God. Surely, God wants us to be well. He wants us to glorify Him for the good things He does for us. For this reason, the Lord Yeshua could not wait any longer, even though He was teaching at the time, to set the woman free from her bondage.

Verse 14

The synagogue official became indignant that the Lord had healed on a Sabbath. Fearing that more people were going to want to get healed; and that attention would shift from him and other officials to this new way, he made an announcement for the people to come another day to be healed.

He never spoke directly to the person he was accusing of breaking the law or being at work. In any case, to be at work meant to do business that earned you an income. The Lord was, therefore, not working; He was merely releasing the poor woman from her adverse condition. Why wait for tomorrow to relieve someone of their burden when it can be done right away?

Verses 15-16

One of the striking things that people did not fully realise about the Lord Yeshua at the time was that the Lord knew them intimately. He knew their culture, habits and reasoning. But they did not know this of Him. So, when in verse 15 the Lord called them hypocrites, He did so because He knew what they would do in their own circumstances. Almost like saying to them, "Raise up your hands, anyone among you, if you would rather take your problems home on a Sabbath, than get rid of them here and now."

He actually gave examples of what work they had done before on Sabbath days with their oxen and with their donkeys. These could also have been construed as breaking the law but they were not. Actually, these acts did not constitute going to the farm or doing work with the animals for profit. Taking the animals out on a Sabbath in order that they might find pasture and water was a good thing to do. It showed that the people were treating the animals in a humane way and the Lord did not chastise them for that.

However, He called them hypocrites for the unkind and unsympathetic way they treated their fellow human beings.

In verse 16, the Lord reminded His accusers that the woman in question was a daughter of Abraham. In other words, she was a "daughter of promise," unlike the donkeys and oxen. If we could have sympathy on animals that have no promise of God, why can't we do more for the children of faith?

For how long had the woman been saying, "Lord, why me?" She probably was not the worst sinner in the land. Were the synagogue officials better than her in the presence of God? Lord, why her? Wasn't it the same grace of God that the officials had?

Verse 17

I am sure the Lord was not out to humiliate the officials. It was the officials that wanted to put the Lord on the spot by indirectly accusing Him of being a false teacher. The crowd, however, loved what they heard from the Lord and could not contain their joy. "The entire multitude was rejoicing over all the glorious things being done by Him" (NASB).

There was no need for the woman to come back another day. There was no need for her to make a separate appointment for special deliverance. God is at work at all times and now is the time for you to be delivered. Right now! You are more valuable to God than the most valuable animal on the earth, and your healing is to you as bread from a father is to his children. Claim it, child of God, and let no man put you off for another day. God is your healer, not man. If man is not ready, God is! Be healed today in the Lord Yeshua's name, Amen. As you claim your healing, shame will go to the devil and all glory will be the Lord's.

Verses 18-22

The above verses tell us what happens when the word of God (the Kingdom of God) gains entry into people's lives. It may just be a simple word that someone hears, but in time it grows and grows, because it has fallen on the garden of a good heart.

It does not have to start big, be well-established or come from a pastor, preacher or a massive Cathedral for it to be effective. No matter how small the word, the hearer always finds peace and rest in it. The word of God proclaimed by the children of God should always provide a haven of peace, love and safety to those who hear it.

The first thing the Lord compared the word of the Kingdom of God to was a haven of peace and rest.

The second comparison was that, no matter how little you have the word of God, which brings the Kingdom of God within you, what you have is so huge that when it starts to manifest in your life, people are going to marvel at you. It will swell, rise, and overshadow all the evil works of darkness around you. So, don't underestimate yourself, child of God. You may start small, but be rest assured that the Kingdom will grow and grow in you. God sows the seed of His Kingdom in our lives for greater and more-lasting benefits. It may start small but it will grow ultimately.

Verse 22 informs us that even though Yeshua was on His way to Jerusalem where He already knew that He would be persecuted, tortured and killed, He was still going from village to village, from city to city, teaching about the Kingdom of God. The Lord Yeshua was here demonstrating how to be persistent; how to keep going on and not give up even at the point of death.

Yeshua demonstrated how we need to be focused in our work for the Lord and not get blown off course by fear or distracted by gossip.

My prayer for you today, is that the Lord will sustain you in times of adversity and calamity; He will preserve you when you encounter the tragedies of this world. Even when you say "Lord, why me?", may you find an adequate response from the Lord to keep you going. No matter how small the word of God you hear at such a time, like a mustard seed, it will help you, grow in you and lift you up to greater heights, in the Lord Yeshua's name, Amen.

Other Books by This Author

CPSIA information can be obtained at www.ICGtesting.com
Printed in the USA
LVOW120037060613

337155LV00001B/31/P